LONGTON HALL
PORCELAIN

The Faber Monographs on Pottery and Porcelain
Edited by W. B. HONEY and ARTHUR LANE

★

ANCIENT AMERICAN POTTERY *by* G. H. S. Bushnell *and* Adrian Digby
EARLY CHINESE POTTERY AND PORCELAIN *by* Basil Gray
LATER CHINESE PORCELAIN *by* Soame Jenyns
COREAN POTTERY *by* W. B. Honey
ENGLISH DELFTWARE *by* F. H. Garner
ENGLISH PORCELAIN OF THE EIGHTEENTH CENTURY *by* J. L. Dixon
MEDIEVAL ENGLISH POTTERY *by* Bernard Rackham
NINETEENTH-CENTURY ENGLISH POTTERY AND PORCELAIN
by Geoffrey Bemrose
ARTIST POTTERS IN ENGLAND *by* Muriel Rose
FRENCH FAÏENCE *by* Arthur Lane
FRENCH PORCELAIN OF THE EIGHTEENTH CENTURY *by* W. B. Honey
GERMAN PORCELAIN *by* W. B. Honey
GREEK POTTERY *by* Arthur Lane
EARLY ISLAMIC POTTERY *by* Arthur Lane
ITALIAN MAIOLICA *by* Bernard Rackham
ITALIAN PORCELAIN *by* Arthur Lane
LONGTON HALL PORCELAIN *by* Bernard Watney
MING POTTERY AND PORCELAIN *by* Soame Jenyns
ORIENTAL BLUE-AND-WHITE *by* Sir Harry Garner
ROMAN POTTERY *by* R. J. Charleston
EARLY STAFFORDSHIRE POTTERY *by* Bernard Rackham
WEDGWOOD WARE *by* W. B. Honey
WORCESTER PORCELAIN *by* Franklin A. Barrett

in preparation

ENGLISH CREAM COLOURED EARTHENWARE *by* Donald Towner
LATER ISLAMIC POTTERY: PERSIA, SYRIA, EGYPT AND TURKEY
by Arthur Lane
HISPANO-MORESQUE POTTERY *by* Arthur Lane
CHELSEA PORCELAIN *by* J. L. Dixon
SCANDINAVIAN FAÏENCE AND PORCELAIN *by* R. J. Charleston
JAPANESE PORCELAIN *by* Soame Jenyns
JAPANESE POTTERY *by* Soame Jenyns
EUROPEAN PORCELAIN FIGURES *by* Arthur Lane
BOW PORCELAIN *by* J. L. Dixon
CHINESE CELADON WARES *by* G. M. Gompertz

★

OTHER TITLES TO FOLLOW
Edited by ARTHUR LANE

A. *Figure of the Duke of Brunswick on horseback*
Late period. Height 8⅗in. British Museum
See page 44

LONGTON HALL
PORCELAIN

by
BERNARD WATNEY

FABER AND FABER
24 Russell Square
London

First published in mcmlvii
by Faber and Faber Limited
24 Russell Square London W.C.1
Printed in Great Britain by
R. MacLehose and Company Limited
The University Press Glasgow

To
JOSEPHINE

'Time's wheel runs back or stops:
Potter and clay endure'

ROBERT BROWNING

FOREWORD

After sweeping Germany and France, the passion for making porcelain reached England shortly before 1750. Obscurity still surrounds the circumstances in which seven factories were founded in as many years. Chelsea, Bow, Derby, and Worcester were successful; Limehouse and Bristol failed almost at once; and the very existence of Longton Hall in Staffordshire was forgotten until its gradual 'rediscovery' through the researches of collectors in modern times. Before Dr. Watney began his fruitful inquiries it was believed that this factory only operated between 1752 and 1758. By brilliant detective work he has tracked down important original documents concerning the management of the factory, and discovered through excavation the actual site of the works. He is now able to show that the enterprise began as early as 1750, if not before, making the primitive 'snowman' figures whose origin has hitherto been unexplained. He gives here, for the first time, a wholly convincing analysis of its artistic development until financial failure overtook it in 1760. Many of its useful wares are shown to have been wrongly attributed to other factories. The attractive figures and groups were modelled with a sense of style well in advance of their time. Indeed the factory represents a remarkable pioneering attempt to introduce porcelain into the stronghold of the English earthenware industry, many years before the new material found general acceptance there.

ARTHUR LANE

ACKNOWLEDGEMENTS

The author wishes to express his grateful acknowledgement to the Staff of the Public Record Office, the District Probate Registry at Birmingham, the Society of Genealogists, the William Salt Library, and the Borthwick Institute of Historical Research.

He is particularly obliged to Mr. Jack Firmin whose ready co-operation resulted in the discovery of the Longton Hall agreements which were at once made freely available for use in this study. It has been a privilege to write under the editorship of Mr. Arthur Lane, whose brilliant insight and scrupulous care have been of great assistance in the preparation of this monograph. Mr. A. J. B. Kiddell has given valuable and constructive advice and criticism, and Mr. T. G. Martin has ungrudgingly applied his wide general knowledge of ceramics whilst reading the manuscript and proofs.

Museum authorities, especially Mr. Geoffrey Bemrose, Mr. Arthur Lane, Mr. F. S. Stonebridge, and Mr. Hugh Tait, have shown great patience and courtesy in complying with many requests.

A special word of thanks is due to kind friends in America who have generously supplied many important illustrations, in particular to Mr. and Mrs. Sigmund Katz. On this side of the Atlantic English collectors have been of the utmost assistance, notably Mr. Ernest Allman, Mr. Tom Burn, Mr. L. Spillman, Dr. and Mrs. Statham, and Mr. Aubrey Toppin, *York Herald*.

The Author's indebtedness to many antique dealers is expressed in the plate captions. He is especially grateful to Mr. A. F. Green, Mr. H. Longden, Mr. John Perkins, Mr. George Savage, Mr. and Mrs. J. Smith, Mr. Graham Thomas, Mr. and Mrs. Tilley, the Directors of Winifred Williams and Mrs. Charles Woollett.

Finally, his thanks are due to Miss C. Tucker who typed the manuscript in her spare time.

CONTENTS

ILLUSTRATIONS

COLOUR PLATES

MONOCHROME PLATES
at the end of the book

ILLUSTRATIONS

(Continued)

NOTE

Mr. and Mrs. Katz have generously granted permission to illustrate the important Jacobite group as the first monochrome plate. However, they do not necessarily agree with the 'snowman' attribution, and are anxious that the other side of the argument should be put on record. It is pointed out that there are some strong similarities to 'triangle period' Chelsea, both in fluorescence (confirmed by Alex Lewis and George Savage) and chemical analysis which was undertaken by Dr. W. H. Webb. It is considered possible that the stylistic resemblance to Staffordshire pottery figures could be accounted for by the presence of Staffordshire potters at Chelsea.

On the other hand the 'snowman' attribution is based on style, the crudeness of potting, and the quality of the paste and glaze. The fluorescence of 'snowmen' and glassy Chelsea porcelains can be almost identical, and their chemical analyses very close. See pages 22, 26 to 29.

INTRODUCTION

On the 8th of September 1760, two different provincial newspapers carried notices relating to the porcelain factory at Longton Hall; one was the final confirmation that the proprietors had dissolved their partnership;[1] the other reported that the stock of the factory was to be sold at Salisbury on the 16th of the month.[2] The sale lasted five days, for, as stated in the advertisement, there were 'upwards of ninety thousand pieces' made up into large lots to be sold 'without reserve or the least addition'.

The Longton Hall factory had been in existence for only ten years when it ended in financial failure and its memory was soon almost completely obliterated by the rising industrial prosperity at Burslem and other neighbouring towns. However, some knowledge of it lingered in Staffordshire among the potters, enabling William Pitt, fifty-seven years later, to piece together a few facts concerning the factory and its manager, William Littler.[3] William Pitt's *Topographical History of Staffordshire* was published in 1817, and although his account is not quoted to any extent by later authorities it is more accurate than that of Simeon Shaw, who wrote his book[4] twelve years afterwards. Having discussed Littler's important innovations as a salt-glaze potter Pitt states that: 'About 1750 he (Littler) left Burslem and commenced a porcelain manufactory at Longton, near Stoke. He so far succeeded as to excite the astonishment of the potters; but it proved an unprofitable article, and the manufacture of it was discontinued. Littler sustained some heavy losses and sold his estate at Brownhills in the parish of Burslem.' Pitt adds: 'Specimens of this porcelain are preserved, which in body, glaze, and enamel, may be considered as excellent for that day.'

Shaw's account is largely a copy of Pitt's description, but some of his additions are inaccurate; and his mention of a Dr. Mills as Littler's chief potter and modeller remains unsubstantiated. Shaw states that: 'The specimens, which are well calculated to deceive the eye of the spectator, are cylindrical cups, with handles showing some taste, a

---

[1] *Aris's Birmingham Gazette.*   [2] *The Salisbury Journal.*
[3] Pitt used an alternative spelling of Littlor, and William Littler's father spelt his name Littleor in his will.
[4] *History of the Staffordshire Potteries*, 1829.

tolerable glaze, and enamelled with flowers, but there are many specks, and the whole has a greyish hue, yet they are calculated to surprise his fellows, by their similarity to foreign porcelain in body, glaze, shapes, and enamelling.' From these accounts it appears that both Pitt and Shaw were well acquainted with this porcelain. The same is true of John Ward[1] who describes these wares as 'some highly transparent and beautiful specimens'. On another page Ward suggests, rather wistfully, that: 'They would certainly have won their way in after times.'

William Evans in his rare book, *The Art and History of the Pottery Business*, 1846, mentions Littler only as a salt-glaze potter, possibly because it was this more successful branch of the potter's craft that was emphasized by earlier writers.

It was now left to collectors and antiquarians not directly associated with Staffordshire to rediscover the existence of the Longton factory, and to identify its productions. The first step in this direction was taken in 1862 when Sir Wollaston Franks, one of the foremost pioneer collectors of his time, exhibited at Worcester[2] 'three specimens of a rare English manufacture of porcelain', attributed to an unknown factory. These are described in the catalogue as bearing the crossed 'L' mark with three dots beneath it. 'The prevalent colour is a brilliant blue; one of the examples exhibited was a leaf-shaped dish, in form similar to those frequently made at Chelsea; also a large plate, and a bowl and cover formed of overlapping leaves, some of them of the peculiar brilliant blue already noticed, decorated with white enamel; the others white and painted with flowers enclosed within floral wreaths.' All three specimens are now in the British Museum.

In 1878 Llewellyn Jewitt produced his book[3] which has been the main foundation of all later English ceramic studies. In his reference to the Longton Hall porcelain factory he quotes Shaw and Ward, and goes on to state that 'some specimens of Littler's porcelain are preserved in private collections, and one or two are in the Hanley Museum'; he adds that one of these latter pieces bears a certificate of authenticity in Enoch Wood's handwriting.[4] Jewitt also mentions two agreements dated the 27th of September 1755, and the 1st of January 1756, in which William Duesbury[5] is described as living at Longton Hall and 'of Longton in ye County of Stafford, Enameller'. This is the

---

[1] *History of the Borough of Stoke-upon-Trent*, 1843.

[2] At a meeting of the Archaeological Institute.

[3] *The Ceramic Art of Great Britain*, 2 vols.

[4] This is the first reference to the Hanley tea-caddy now considered to have a spurious documentation and to be of Liverpool origin.

[5] A person of outstanding importance in eighteenth-century English porcelain manufacture at Derby and elsewhere.

first evidence of Duesbury's connection with the Longton Hall factory.

The next major advance was made in 1881 when J. E. Nightingale published the results of his painstaking researches.[1] He suggested that the three specimens isolated by Franks corresponded with the types of ware mentioned in the London newspaper advertisements of the 12th and 25th of April 1757, which he had recently discovered. Nightingale was also able to find other advertisements ranging in date from July 1752, to June 1758, some in *Aris's Birmingham Gazette* and others in the *London Public Advertiser*. This brilliant detective work laid the foundations upon which William Bemrose was able to produce his monograph on Longton Hall porcelain in 1906, which held the field for twenty years.

Bemrose's contribution was threefold: he showed the relationship between the salt-glaze wares and the porcelain made by William Littler; drew attention to the London work-books of William Duesbury in which Littler and Co. are mentioned; and was also largely responsible for separating Longton figures from those of other factories.[2]

Since Bemrose published his two books modern connoisseurship, aided by scientific methods, has been able to build up a more accurate picture of the porcelain manufactured at Longton Hall, and it is now accepted that about seventy of the pieces (mostly domestic ware) illustrated in *Longton Hall Porcelain* are wrongly attributed and are mainly of Liverpool or Derby origin.

In recent years some further significant facts have come to light largely as the result of research by members of the English Ceramic Circle. One of the founder members, Mrs. Donald MacAlister, contributed two important papers[3] describing an early group of white figures (nicknamed 'snowmen'). She linked these figures with the early wares which Dr. Pococke had seen at Newcastle-under-Lyme in July 1750. She showed their strong Staffordshire associations, and suggested that these primitive figures might have been amongst the first products of the Longton factory.

Mr. A. J. B. Kiddell[4] discovered an isolated notice in the *General Evening Post* of the 30th of September to the 3rd of October 1758, announcing the opening of a Longton China Warehouse at the corner of St. Paul's Churchyard next to Watling Street. More recently Mr. Geoffrey Wills[5] discovered a further notice in the same paper for the

[1] *Contributions Towards the History of Early English Porcelain.*
[2] Appendix to *Bow, Chelsea and Derby Porcelain*, 1898.
[3] *Trans. E.P.C.*, No. 11, 1929, and *Trans. E.C.C.*, No. 1, 1933.
[4] *Trans. E.P.C.*, No. 111, 1931.
[5] *Apollo*, vol. LX, August 1954.

14th of July 1759, stating that the co-partnership between Messrs. Banks and Robertson of the Staffordshire Warehouse in St. Paul's Churchyard had been dissolved by mutual consent on the 24th of June 1759, and that Mr. Robertson had subsequently opened a large warehouse at the east corner of St. Paul's Churchyard next to Watling Street.

In 1933 Mr. Kiddell[1] reported the discovery of three announcements in the *Birmingham Gazette* for the year 1760. The first was dated the 9th of June and stated that on the 23rd of May 1760, Mr. Robert Charlesworth had dissolved the Longton Hall partnership pursuant to their articles and agreements. The second dated the 30th of June was an objection by William Littler and Co. affirming that it was not in Robert Charlesworth's power to dissolve the partnership without the consent of the rest of the partners. In the last announcement on the 8th of September Samuel Firmin 'esteems' that the partnership was dissolved on the 23rd of May pursuant to a notice sent him by Robert Charlesworth.

This discovery was the most valuable documentary addition since Nightingale, the new names supplying clues which have been followed up with most interesting and far reaching results by the writer of the present monograph.

*　　*　　*　　*　　*

This study was begun in what seemed at first to be an ambitious attempt to solve some of the outstanding problems concerning the Longton factory. On the documentary side uncertainty existed as to the owners of the Hall in the eighteenth century, and very little was known about the place prior to the factory's existence. In this connection genealogical research gave fruitful results.

Uncertainty also existed as to when or how the factory began, and here the newly-discovered factory agreements showed that William Jenkinson was the key to the problem. Furthermore the agreements supply conclusive evidence of the factory's uninterrupted life-span and they help to explain the final press notices of 1760.

On the material side there was uncertainty of attribution of existing pieces to Longton; hitherto much had been reasonable conjecture based on stylistic comparison. As Longton is in the salt-glaze and earthenware-producing 'Potteries' and Littler was originally an 'earth potter', it seemed reasonable to assume that early porcelain with a Staffordshire character (that is, corresponding with pottery models and shapes) could be credited with a Longton origin.

In the past an application of scientific methods to the study of

---

[1] *Trans. E.C.C.*, No. 1.

INTRODUCTION

Longton porcelain had been attempted but not taken very far. The present approach incorporates more intense scientific enquiries based especially on fluorescence tests[1] and chemical tests, both these being valuable ancillary aids. Careful attention to the visual appearance of paste and glaze has nevertheless remained a major criterion, especially in the isolation of the later blue-and-white wares, a task which had already been begun in an understandably cautious manner by W. B. Honey.[2] Furthermore, intensified stylistic comparisons have played an important part where possible confusions arose with early Derby, Liverpool, Worcester or even Bow and Lowestoft.

The most conclusive argument in favour of a Longton origin for the disputed types would naturally be the discovery on the site of the old Longton works of recognizable fragments. This necessitated excavations, and the resulting finds have established several important identifications, chiefly amongst the domestic wares of the middle and late periods, but fortunately including two of the earliest figures.

Lastly, in the light of the available evidence an attempt has been made to classify the factory's products in a definite chronological order.

[1] Under invisible ultra-violet light porcelain has the property of fluorescing; that is, emitting comparatively weak visible light. The colour of the fluorescence depends on a number of complicated factors such as molecular structure of the porcelain constituents. In general the early porcelains show characteristic fluorescences for each particular factory. Two types of ultra-violet light are used, known as 'long' and 'short' waves. The present writer favours 'short' waves for a study of Longton porcelain.

[2] *Old English Porcelain*, 1948, *Plate* 67A.

1

THE MANOR OF LONGTON

'The Potteries' in North Staffordshire once consisted of five separate towns—Tunstall, Burslem, Hanley, Stoke and Longton. After the pottery industry entered on its great expansion towards the end of the eighteenth century the open country between these places rapidly disappeared, and today the original Five Towns with some others have merged into the sprawling urban area that forms the municipality of Stoke-on-Trent. Longton is the southernmost member of this federation.

'The Vill of Longton' already existed in the thirteenth century when it was mentioned in a legal document;[1] at that time it was held in lease from the Manor of Newcastle-under-Lyme, a town some five miles to the north-west.

John Ward, writing in 1843,[2] confirms that 'the Manor of Longton has continued down to the present time to be held under the seigniory of Newcastle and the Duchy of Lancaster', and an enquiring visitor to Longton in the middle of the eighteenth century would certainly have been informed of its dependence on Newcastle. Thus Dr. Richard Pococke, in a letter to his mother dated the 14th of July 1750,[3] reported that 'Newcastle-on-Line' was then 'the market town and Capital of the Pottery villages; there are some few Potters here, and one I visited, whom I saw at Limehouse,[4] who promised to make the best china ware, but disagreed with his employers, and has a great quantity made here for the oven'. This sentence is somewhat ambiguous but in apparently placing this china-maker's activities at Newcastle itself Pococke may have been guilty of a slip of the pen, or, at least, of the memory—he had passed on to Boulness near Carlisle

[1] *Testa de Nevill* described by William Pitt, *A Topographical History of Staffordshire*, 1817, p. 354.

[2] *History of the Borough of Stoke-upon-Trent.*

[3] British Museum Add. MS. 15,800. The Camden Society's printed version of *Pococke's Tours* (1888-9) includes corrections in the MSS. which have been omitted here as they appear to be by a later hand.

[4] A poorly-documented, short-lived china factory in the East End of London which apparently became bankrupt in 1748 and is important for its Bristol and Staffordshire connections.

by the time he wrote the letter, and in his next paragraph by con-
fusing 'Audley Green' with Hanley Green he showed that he had
no clear idea in retrospect of the location of at least one of the pottery
villages. It is now generally accepted that the new porcelain factory
seen by Pococke in 1750 was actually at Longton Hall, especially as
the majority of the factory's advertisements were later to describe its
situation as being near Newcastle. Furthermore we have no evidence
of china being made elsewhere in 'the Potteries' at that time.

Up to the present day the Longton estate[1] has stood rather outside
the area where the pot-making industry was chiefly concentrated.
It is true that Thomas Whieldon (1719–95) had his famous earthenware pottery at Fenton Low not far away, but it is puzzling nevertheless that such an isolated place should have been chosen for the site of
the first china factory in Staffordshire. The following particulars concerning the past owners of Longton Hall may help to shed some light
on this problem.

Ward states that the Manor of Longton was once the property of
the Lords Foley, who early in the eighteenth century sold it to the
ancestors of the Rev. Obadiah Lane, from whose representatives it was
purchased in 1777 by Sir John Edensor Heathcote, Knight. As a
confirmation of Ward's statement a certain Richard Foley is mentioned in Burke's *Peerage* as owning Longton Hall in the seventeenth
century, and his name also appears in a seventeenth-century document referring to the mining of coal in the Longton area.[2] He was
the son of Richard Foley of Stourbridge and was, like his father, a
famous ironmaster.

J. E. Nightingale,[3] in attempting to review the past history of
Longton Hall, quotes the Rev. Stebbing Shaw about the Weedons
and the Floyers of Longdon Hall and it is obvious that he has con-
fused that place, which is near Lichfield, with Longton Hall, which is
in the parish of Stoke-upon-Trent.

Ward's statement referred to above was nearer to the truth, as
there was a grant of Arms to a certain Obadiah Lane dated the 11th
of February 1703–4, where he is described as being of Longton and
Lane End. In his will[4] dated the 1st of September 1706, made at
Bath in Somerset and proved on the 17th of March 1708–9, Obadiah
Lane is described as being of Normicote Grange in the county of
Staffordshire, Gentleman. In this he stated that he had provided for
his son, Nathaniel Lane, in his marriage settlement, and it is likely

---

[1] The Hall itself was demolished in 1939.
[2] Heathcote Collection, William Salt Library, Stafford.
[3] *Contributions towards the History of Early English Porcelain*, 1881.
[4] P.C.C. Folio 59 *Barrett*.

that he was referring to the Longton estates. His will contains a description of his many iron works, including furnaces, forges, slitting mills and plating works in the counties of Stafford, Gloucester, Chester and Denbigh, all of which he left to his wife, Anne Lane. His eldest son, Nathaniel, was an ironmaster like his father, and when he died at Longton Hall on the 1st of November 1720,[1] an inventory of his estate showed that the value of his 'stock in the Iron Trades and Partnership and Iron Stone got and not melted down was £1015.19.0'. Nathaniel's eldest son died as a young man, and his son, Obadiah (II), inherited the Longton estates. Obadiah (II) was born about 1708 and educated at Westminster School. We know that he was 'of Longton' from 1732 to 1749 as he is so described in the baptismal entries of his children in the Stoke-upon-Trent registers. In a deed of lease of some property in Trentham 'save the getting of iron stone, coals and lime' to a certain Thomas Wolfe dated the 1st of August 1752,[2] he is described as of Birmingham. In his will dated the 2nd of December 1755, and proved on the 13th of December 1757,[3] he is also described as 'of Birmingham in the county of Warwick, Esquire'. These dates are important as they show that Obadiah (II) Lane was not living at Longton during the time the Longton factory was in existence. Some time before 1751 he had let the Hall to a certain William Jenkinson for twenty-five pounds per annum.[4] We shall see later that William Jenkinson was not only connected with the mining industry but that he was also the founder of the Longton porcelain manufactory.

One of Obadiah (II) Lane's sons was also called Obadiah (III) and he inherited the Longton estates whilst the porcelain factory was still in existence. He was baptized in 1733 at Stoke-on-Trent and admitted a sizar at Emmanuel College, Cambridge, on the 25th of November 1751. He was ordained deacon (Ely) on the 28th of December 1756, and was Prebend of Lichfield (Gaia-Minor) from 1767 to 1780.[5] He retained possession of the Longton Manor until his death in 1780, and in his will made at Chester, dated the 20th of September 1779,[6] he gave directions for the Manor of Longton to be sold after his death by his executors, John Crewe of Bolesworth Castle, his relative, and James Tomkinson, the younger, of Dorfold. A deed in the Heathcote Collection shows that these two men had been made trustees of the Longton Estate on the 20th of September 1773, and it mentions that

[1] Will proved at Lichfield 6th December 1720.
[2] Heathcote Collection, William Salt Library.
[3] P.C.C. Folio 363 *Herring*.
[4] It is disappointing that this deed of lease is missing from the Heathcote Collection.
[5] *Alumni Cantabrigienses*, Part 1, Vol. III.
[6] P.C.C. Folio 364 *Collins*.

one of the Foleys, Thomas Foley of Stoke Court and Whetley Court, still owned some land in the Manor of Longton at that time.

Sir John Edensor Heathcote, a wealthy ironmaster, evidently leased Longton Hall in the 1770's but did not purchase it until after the death of the Rev. Obadiah (III) Lane in 1780. In a letter dated the 17th of December 1777, Josiah Wedgwood writes to Bentley[1] that Mr. Heathcote 'is repairing Longton Hall in our neighbourhood and wishes to have one of our chimney pieces'. (Two such chimney pieces were actually made and fitted,[2] and it is interesting to recall that the same chimney pieces were exhibited at South Kensington many years later before going to America.) However, the Heathcotes not only repaired the Hall, but they also built their magnificent coach-houses and stables on top of the Longton porcelain factory site; these buildings are still standing today.

Ward described Longton Hall as being in the style of Queen Anne and 'situated in the midst of a well wooded domain of considerable extent and beauty', and his remarks are confirmed by an engraving of the Hall after a drawing by Lady Elizabeth, second wife of Richard Heathcote, who was the son of Sir John Heathcote.

This secluded place had provided the secrecy necessary for a porcelain manufactory and its association with the mining industries had brought about two very important conditions: a cheap source of fuel, and the technical knowledge of controlling high temperatures in the blast furnaces. Unlimited supplies of coal were readily available near at hand, and its cheapness is shown by the fact that in Dr. Plot's time[3] coal was about one shilling and fourpence a ton, and even a hundred years later the price had risen to only four shillings and sixpence a ton.

Here then were convenient quarters for someone with technical ability and a recipe for porcelain, and the necessary determination to overcome the difficulty of firing it at the high temperature required, using coal instead of wood.

[1] Elizabeth Meteyard, *The Life of Josiah Wedgwood*, 1865, Vol. II, p. 373.
[2] *Old Wedgwood*, pamphlet by Frederick Rathbone, 1893.
[3] *The Natural History of Staffordshire*, 1686.

2

THE PROPRIETORS
OF THE FACTORY

Before attempting to explore the Longton site it was decided that a serious effort should be made to obtain more information concerning the proprietors of the factory. Documentary researches clearly indicated that further clues were unlikely to be forthcoming from a study of the Lane family history. Previous writers had concentrated on the part played by Littler, but no one had yet made use of Kiddell's discovery in 1933 of two other partners, Robert Charlesworth and Samuel Firmin. The Lichfield Calendars[1] supplied no reference to Firmin and none of the Charlesworths listed appeared to have any connection with the factory. The next line of approach as planned would have involved a systematic search through the Calendars of the Prerogative Court of Canterbury at Somerset House. But through a lucky chance in February 1955, this procedure was cut short by a reference to the London telephone directory which listed no less than twenty Firmins living in the London area. The first one of these to be visited, Mr. Jack Firmin, is the managing director of an old-established firm of button-makers, and it was soon evident that he had had an ancestor in the same business named Samuel Firmin. Impressed with the importance of further investigations, Mr. Firmin kindly permitted a search through two old deed-boxes in his cellars. In one of these boxes, amongst a pile of eighteenth-century documents, the author was extremely fortunate to discover two original Longton Hall indentures which had remained unrecognized for nearly two hundred years.

The earlier indenture, dated the 25th of August 1753, refers to a previous indenture dated the 7th of October 1751, of which no copy has yet been traced. The later indenture dated the 1st of September 1755 is endorsed by two supplemental agreements dated the 20th of

[1] Before 1858 the proving of wills was a function of the Ecclesiastical Courts, the Pottery area coming within the jurisdiction of Lichfield. The Prerogative Court of Canterbury dealt with wills connected with property in more than one jurisdiction.

10

October 1756, and the 1st of October 1757.[1] We are informed that the first indenture (7th October 1751) was made between William Jenkinson, William Nicklin and William Littler, also that 'William Jenkinson had Obtained the Art Secret or Mystery' of making porcelain in imitation of china ware and that he had rented the Longton premises from Obadiah Lane sometime before 1751. Prior to this first partnership Jenkinson had established a factory with sufficient output, probably including figures, (see the reference to models), for his porcelain to be mentioned in the first agreement as part of his assets.

William Jenkinson is a new name in ceramics and his attempt to make porcelain was successful largely because he was able to adapt his technical knowledge derived from his interest in the mining industries, and because of his appreciation of the fact that coal could be used as a cheap fuel to fire the kilns.[2] In his will dated the 24th of August 1771,[3] he is described as 'late of Oswestry in the county of Salop but now of Lambeth in the county of Surrey, Esquire'. He refers to his invention of an 'engine for raising water out of coal mines or any other mines' for which he had obtained a patent enrolled on the 5th of April 1769, and to which patent is attached a signed coloured drawing.[4] Jenkinson was unable to exploit this invention himself because he had been smitten with a stroke. But he intended that his niece, Phoebe Meir, a spinster living near Stoke-on-Trent, and the children of his sister Ann Humphries of Portsmouth, together with a certain John Dovaston of Oswestry and James Barker of Lambeth, were to share any future profits of his invention.

He also related how he 'sold to the Right Honourable Lord Verney the Honor of Pontefract', for which it was agreed that his Lordship should pay him an annuity of one hundred and fifty pounds during Jenkinson's lifetime; or in case the benefit and interest arising from the said manor should exceed the sum of two hundred pounds a year, then it was agreed that his Lordship should pay him a yearly sum of two hundred pounds during his natural life.

William Jenkinson was obviously an influential person. He is described as a 'gentleman' in the Longton agreements, and as 'Esquire' in his will. But nothing has yet been discovered about his early life, and no help has been obtained from the Oswestry registers or from the published histories of Pontefract. A certain similarity can be noted between William Jenkinson and Benjamin Lund, another early speculator in porcelain who founded the first Bristol factory at Low-

[1] See Appendix A.
[2] No other contemporary porcelain factory is known to have used coal at this early date.
[3] P.C.C. Folio 410 *Trevor*.
[4] Patent Rolls P.R.O.

din's glasshouse in 1749.[1] Lund was probably the person referred to by Dr. Pococke, in describing his visit to Bristol, as 'one of the principal manufacturers at Limehouse which failed'.[2] Lund was originally a brass-founder and copper-merchant, and Jenkinson too appears to have had mining and probably metallurgical interests. It is almost certain that Jenkinson, like Lund, obtained his secret recipe for porcelain in London, the natural centre from which foreign-inspired fashions were diffused. (The earliest English porcelain factories, Chelsea, Bow and Limehouse, had all started in London before 1750.) There is circumstantial evidence to suggest that Jenkinson, like Lund, had obtained his knowledge of porcelain through the abortive Limehouse venture. For Pococke recognized the porcelain-maker working at 'Newcastle-on-Line' in July 1750[3] as a man whom he had seen previously at Limehouse, where he 'disagreed with his employers'. This man is unlikely to have been Jenkinson, for if a man of Jenkinson's social position had been actively connected with the Limehouse factory, he would have been on at least an equal footing with Lund. The man whom Pococke saw was only an employee, working, we presume, at Longton Hall for Jenkinson.

Jenkinson's interest in porcelain was short-lived and the second agreement (25th August 1753) concerns the sale of his shares mostly to a new partner, Nathaniel Firmin. William Jenkinson then withdraws from the partnership 'for divers other good causes and valuable considerations', and he promises not to make the porcelain or to divulge the secret of its composition during the remainder of the term of fourteen years from the date of the first agreement. After leaving Longton Hall it is probable that he moved to Oswestry, and later to Lambeth, where he died. There is now no trace of his grave in St. Mary's Churchyard at Lambeth where he was buried on the 16th of October 1771.

William Littler is described as 'late of Hanley Green in the Parish of Stoke-upon-Trent, Earth Potter'. His father, William Littler, was also a potter who owned Bourne Meadow with the appurtenances in the Parish of Burslem, and he left this property to his wife, Sarah, in his will dated the 20th of May 1724.[4] He mentions two potters: John Cartleitch of Brownhills and Ralph Shawe, junior, of Burslem, who were to manage his estate for the benefit of his children in case of his wife's remarriage or death. William Littler, senior, had married Sarah Shawe, probably Ralph Shawe's sister, at Burslem on the 3rd of

[1] Aubrey J. Toppin, *Trans. E.C.C.*, Vol. 3, Part 3.
[2] British Museum Add. MS. 15,800.
[3] See passage already quoted above, pp. 6-7.
[4] Proved at Lichfield, 23rd April 1730.

April 1719, and in May 1724, he describes her as 'being great with child'; six months later, on the 1st of December, their son, William Littler, was baptized at Burslem. William Littler, senior, was buried at Burslem on the 12th of September 1729, leaving a young family of four children to be brought up by their mother.

At the time of the first agreement (7th October 1751) William Littler was only twenty-six years of age, and it seems rather unlikely that he could have been the mysterious potter from Limehouse. In the first place, he is not credited in the agreements with any prior knowledge of the porcelain manufacture; secondly, William Pitt implies that Littler was fully occupied with new methods of salt-glaze production before becoming the manager of the Longton factory;[1] however, a Limehouse connection for William Littler cannot definitely be ruled out. Dr. Pococke refers to the potter from Limehouse making 'what he calls Japann'd ware, and of this he has made many boxes for ladies toilets and several other things'.[2] It is significant that the Longton agreements contain further references to the decorating of porcelain by japanning. Pitt describes how William Littler, in conjunction with his brother-in-law Aaron Wedgwood, had invented a liquid glaze, for improving the appearance of salt-glaze wares, containing flint and clay as used for the pottery body as well as ground *zaffer*. The unfired vessels were dipped into this before glazing with salt in the usual manner. Because of the fluxing effect of the cobalt this produced a fine, smooth, glossy surface quite free from the usual pitting of salt glaze. These distinctive wares, Pitt adds, possessed 'all the beauty of the finest lapis lazuli; others from the admixture of a small proportion of manganese have the appearance of the finest oriental lapis lazuli. These articles were further ornamented by enamelling, gilding etc.'. This type of opaque blue ground with superadded gilding and enamelling, including the rare use of a distinctive white enamel, was adapted by Littler for the decoration of early Longton porcelain, and it is reasonable to assume that this is the process referred to above as japanning. Some of the earliest pieces of Longton porcelain are decorated in this manner and it is highly probable that William Jenkinson sought William Littler's advice on the technique of potting and its decoration before the first agreement was signed.

The second agreement (25th August 1753) mentions that Littler was then married, and the third agreement (1st September 1755) reveals that for her services in the management of the factory his wife, Jane, was to be paid one guinea a week.

[1] *A Topographical History of Staffordshire*, 1817.
[2] British Museum Add. MS. 15,800.

He and his wife promised to 'employ the utmost application and diligence in the conduct, business and management of the factory' and not to live away from Longton Hall without the consent of the other partners. The agreement concerns them especially where it lays down that the books of accounts must be kept up-to-date and always available for inspection; furthermore, the factory's secrets were to be made known to the other partners. Another important condition was that nobody could be employed by Littler at the factory without the consent of the other proprietors. A certain John Hayfield is mentioned as the only painter then working at Longton Hall, and for his services he was to be paid one guinea a week. If this artist neglected his work Littler could discharge him and engage another approved person in his stead, 'employing one painter and no more at the same time'. John Hayfield would doubtless have had a number of enamellers working under him, leaving only the more important pieces for his personal decoration. This conjecture is strengthened by a study of the Longton porcelain produced at that time, which suggests that all the more ambitious painting was done by one hand. Favourite subjects were romantic landscapes and harbour scenes, often including castles and churches.

A schedule[1] attached to the third agreement contains a list of outstanding debts to a number of tradesmen and factory employees, many of whom, such as Ridgway, Baddeley and Bagnall, bear well-known local names. 'Mr.' suggests someone of superior status, and it is a nice touch that Mr. Duesbury should be mentioned although the money owing to him 'for work' had presumably been paid. Others who apparently worked in the factory are a Mr. Derby, and Hollins and Mountford. Miss Shaw, who was possibly related to Littler, was due to receive a large sum of money, but her duties are not stated. Shop goods, presumably such items as enamel colours and gold, were obtained from Mr. Smallwood, Shaw and Ridgway for £23 3s. 10d. It is possible that the Ridgway referred to was Ralph Ridgway, the master-potter of Chell, who failed in business in 1756, and whose son started a factory in 1792 at Shelton in the premises formerly occupied by Warner Edwards, the celebrated manufacturer of enamel colours.

The sum of £45 11s. 6d. for coals is proof that large quantities were used for firing the wares.[2] Broken glass or cullet was bought from four different people for a total cost of £20 7s. 7½d. The schedule even mentions the brickmaker and the bricklayer who built the kilns. It is probably their sons who are listed in a Staffordshire pottery directory compiled about 1800 as John Hulme, a bricklayer of Lane End, and Richard Hammersley, a brickmaker in Great Fenton. Mr. Charlton

[1] Appendix A.   [2] See p. 61.

14

was evidently the man who distributed the wages, possibly an accounts clerk. His signature appears as a witness to the third agreement together with that of J. Sparrow, an attorney who had previously been apprenticed to William Nicklin.

The Longton factory would almost certainly have failed in 1755 had it not been for the new partner, Robert Charlesworth, who provided ready cash to pay the outstanding debts listed in the schedule, as well as fresh capital to continue production. Nevertheless, William Littler, in spite of his determined efforts, was not successful in making the Longton venture a paying concern; and after another five years, Robert Charlesworth, realizing that there was then no chance of any return for his money, dissolved the partnership on the 23rd of May 1760. However, in defiance of this, William Littler continued production for another few months until the factory's stock was removed to Salisbury for sale.

Simeon Shaw recounts that at some later date Littler became the manager of Messrs. Baddeley and Fletcher's porcelain factory in Shelton. John Baddeley, we are told by Shaw, was the father of two well-known earthenware potters, Ralph and John Baddeley of Shelton. He is probably the person listed as a bankrupt in July 1760, described as John Baddeley, Potter, late of Shelton.[1] Thomas Fletcher of Newcastle-under-Lyme was more fortunate, for he married Elizabeth, daughter and co-heir of John Fenton, and their son, Sir Thomas Fletcher of Betley, became High Sheriff for Staffordshire. It appears that Baddeley and Fletcher fired their porcelain with wood 'because the body would not bear coals', but Shaw seems to contradict this statement, as when actually describing some of this porcelain he notes that 'it is difficult to distinguish it from good blue and white porcelain from Canton; thus suggesting that it was a high-fired ware. If Baddeley and Fletcher did, indeed, make porcelain, it is possible that magnesia was used in the paste, as Mr. Morton Nance discovered a licence dated 1760 which was granted to John Baddeley and William Yates, gentlemen of Newcastle-under-Lyme, to dig and search for soap rock on a part of the Lizard peninsula.[2] Nevertheless, the factory's output was probably on a small scale and lacking in individuality, as none of the wares can at present be identified.

Unfortunately Shaw's statements cannot be accepted without verification from other sources, as a large proportion of his interesting writings contains little more than a grain of truth. A case in point is his description of Littler, poverty-stricken and infirm, dying at a very advanced age in Shelton. It is no doubt true that Littler died a poor

[1] *The Gentleman's Magazine*, Vol. 31, p. 335.
[2] *E.C.C. Trans.*, No. 1, 1933.

man, as no will of his can be traced, but the Burslem registers show that he was buried on the 28th of October 1784, and was not, therefore, over sixty years of age.

The least important of the three original proprietors is William Nicklin. At the outset he held the same number of shares as William Jenkinson, but he took no practical interest in the factory and was what we should nowadays call a sleeping partner. The Nicklins were a large family centred at Tipton in south Staffordshire, with a branch in north Staffordshire, and another in London. The fact that a number of the London Nicklins were buried at Bunhill Fields suggests that they were nonconformists. Many of this family were yeomen, farmers, and tradesmen, others owned coal mines and iron works; but our William Nicklin is described as a gentleman of Newcastle-under-Lyme. A search in the Apprentice Indenture books at the Public Record Office revealed that he was an advocate by profession and had taken an apprentice in 1741 named Randall Colclough for the sum of £105, and, for a similar sum in 1753, he had taken another apprentice named John Sparrow. John Sparrow's signature appears as a witness on the third agreement.

When William Jenkinson sold his shares in 1753 a new partner, Nathaniel Firmin, bought the major part of them. Nathaniel Firmin is described as of the parish of St. Clement Danes in the county of Middlesex, water gilder. I found it possible to trace his connections back through a number of generations, the family being a large one, hailing mainly from Essex and Suffolk. They were mostly churchmen, merchants, and farmers, and many of their number were renowned for their pious and generous acts. Nathaniel's father was the Rev. Giles Firmin of Ovington, who died in 1725.[1] Both Nathaniel's grandfather and great-grandfather had emigrated to America because of their nonconformist faith, and both were named Giles Firmin. His great-grandfather was an apothecary of Sudbury, Suffolk, who died at Boston, Mass., in 1634. His grandfather was a physician who studied at Cambridge University and practised physic both in England and New England, later becoming the vicar of Shalford in Essex. He was the author of several religious books and tracts, and died in April 1697.

Nathaniel Firmin is described as a water gilder in the Longton agreements, but in other documents he is described as a merchant tailor and a button merchant. His own business was carried on 'at the Red Lion over against Norfolk Street in the Strand'. He obtained a Royal Warrant which was renewed for his direct descendents by each successive sovereign from the time of George II to the present day.

Water gilding is likely to have been a method of gilding metals with

[1] P.C.C. Folio 64 *Romney*.

an amalgam of mercury and gold, then known as liquid gold or gold water.[1] Heat was applied to drive off the mercury and the objects were afterwards burnished. However, water gilding is also described in contemporary manuals[2] as an entirely different process for covering wood and stucco with gold leaf without the use of heat. The gold leaf is laid on a moistened sized ground with a squirrel's tail and burnished with a dog's or wolf's tooth or a bloodstone.

It is possible that the Firmins could have given Littler some advice on the technique of gilding, although mercury gilding on porcelain does not appear to have been practised in the Potteries until later in the eighteenth century. The method was apparently first suggested to John Hancock, an employee of Messrs. Turner of Lane End, following a conversation of William Smith of Hanley, 'who possessed the secret of water gilding practised in Birmingham'.[3] Unfired gilding was a common but unsatisfactory feature of the early Longton wares, but about 1754 there was a complete change and from that time onwards gilding was properly fired and burnished.

Just over six months after he was admitted to the Longton partnership Nathaniel Firmin died, and in his will dated the 20th of October, 1753,[4] he left to his son, Samuel, all his 'one fourth part or share' which he purchased from William Jenkinson of the Longton Hall factory 'with all the profits and advantages that doth or may arise from the said factory'. There follow provisos that Nathaniel's brother, sister, daughter and younger son should receive certain benefits from this bequest. He then states that in case his 'one fourth part or share of the Longton Hall factory doth not produce neat and clear profit five hundred pounds a year' then the bequests to his two younger children are to be lessened in the proportion of two-fifths.

Since Nathaniel Firmin expected a fourth part of the shares to yield five hundred pounds it is evident that the total shares were expected to bring in a clear profit of two thousand pounds a year. Subsequent events, however, proved that such large profits were not to be made from this venture.

On the 1st of September 1755, Robert Charlesworth became a partner and the major shareholder. The third agreement and the supplemental agreements make it plain that from that time onwards the continued existence of the Longton factory depended almost entirely upon his financial backing. After 1757, the date of the last supplemental agreement, it appears that the partnership persisted for

[1] W. Salmon, *Polygraphice*, 1685, p. 268.
[2] *Dictionarium Polygraphicum*, second Edition, 1758.
[3] Simeon Shaw, *History of the Staffordshire Potteries*, 1829.
[4] P.C.C. Folio 74 *Pinfold*.

nearly another three years up to the 23rd of May 1760, when Robert Charlesworth sent Samuel Firmin a notice stating that he had dissolved the partnership. Samuel Firmin later published his confirmatory announcement on the 8th of September 1760.

The Rev. Robert Charlesworth, of Bakewell, was educated at Chesterfield and at St. John's College, Cambridge, where he was admitted a pensioner at the age of nineteen in March 1736–7. He was the son of Robert Charlesworth, Gentleman, of Derby, and was born at Castleton about 1717. He was ordained deacon (Lincoln) in 1741 and priest (York) September 1743, and in the same month he became a curate of Birkin in Yorkshire with a salary of fifty-two pounds ten shillings a year. He was lecturer at Halifax from September 1759, to August 1767, when he resigned from this post. In his will executed at Halifax on the 23rd of May 1786, and proved on the 16th of December of the same year,[1] he left over fifteen thousand seven hundred pounds; and in a preliminary draft, which has been preserved, he mentions his lead mines.

In 1758 Dossie wrote that he had seen some kaolin from the Derbyshire mines,[2] and in a recent article[3] Franklin Barrett shows that china clay of a beautiful white colour and steatite or soapstone had been found in the lead mines at Brassington in Derbyshire. It is possible that these mines may have supplied the Longton factory with materials, especially as a certain amount of magnesia is found in chemical analysis of a number of Longton wares. It is also possible that it was because of his ownership of lead mines that Charlesworth first became interested in the Longton factory.

[1] P.C.C. Folio 607 *Norfolk.*
[2] *The Handmaid to the Arts,* Vol. 2, p. 339
[3] *Duesbury and Lead Mining—The Antique Collector,* Vol. 26, No. 4, August 1955.

3

EXCAVATIONS

This was the climax of our research: for two years beforehand information had been slowly accumulating; then came the unexpected discovery of the original Longton agreements, which gave us a few more clues as to the factory's whereabouts, barely a month before our digging operations were to commence. To attempt to excavate alone would have been disastrous, and I needed the companionship and competition provided by someone else who was prepared to work hard. Dr. Geoffrey Blake consented to make the attempt with me, and I was glad that his efforts were rewarded when he found the first fragment of Longton porcelain.

The Longton estate seemed a most unpromising place in which to find the factory site; even today it is rather secluded and aloof. The Hall was demolished in 1939, but, fortunately, a large part of the estate has not yet been incorporated in the built-up area adjacent to it. To the south of the Hall's foundations pasture-land slopes down rather steeply to the Longton Brook, and on the north-east side are the solid red-brick stables standing on somewhat higher ground a stone's throw away. Their blocked-up windows dominate the landscape and have a forbidding look, which brings to mind the words quoted by William Bemrose that 'digging under such unpromising circumstances would be courting failure'. On the far side of these buildings away from the Hall are the sad and all but obliterated remains of gardens, orchards, and carriage drives.

We concentrated our efforts on the north-east side of the Hall's foundations which we decided was the most likely area, partly because of the lie of the land, and also because of the direction of the prevailing winds.

It had been an early Staffordshire practice to build kilns either alongside or close behind potters' houses, as at Shelton Hall; and the Longton agreements suggested that the kilns were no great distance from the Hall in which Littler lived and where the books of accounts were kept. The schedule attached to the third agreement showed that a vast amount of coal was used in the factory, and since we already

19

knew that spacious coal-cellars had existed close behind the Hall near the stables, this furnished another possible clue to the factory's whereabouts.

The stables are situated in the centre of the area we had planned to excavate, and it became increasingly obvious as we proceeded that these large buildings with their cobbled courtyard had been built by Sir John Heathcote on the exact site of the dismantled porcelain factory.

Our trial excavations eventually uncovered the edge of the factory site on the west side of the stables, and the nearer we approached these buildings the larger were the fragments of saggars and other kiln furniture. We also found the commencement of foundations, and more recent excavations have confirmed our belief that kiln foundations extend under the stable buildings.

Some details of our excavations have already been published,[1] but, since then, further material has become available; and the subsequent excavations by the staff of the Hanley Museum are of special interest. These more recent excavations have uncovered foundations which are probably those of an enamel kiln, and the insulating bricks which we had previously discovered appear to have been part of the walls of this structure. These firebricks are hollowed out on one side for better insulation, the other side having a flat glazed surface to face the inside of the muffle kiln. They were cemented together and grooves running round their sides enabled the cementing material to make a better joint between them. A spy-hole cone, complete with its plug, is now in the Hanley Museum together with a number of broken clay firebars and other important evidence of kiln working.

The precise significance of some finds is still in doubt, and in this class are some large glazed tiles, having multiple cylindrical holes just large enough to admit the tip of the little finger, with cruciform mouldings at the bottom of each hole. These holes probably held clay pegs to support wares in the kiln. There were also a few large cylindrical fireclay objects having a dividing lug on top forming two shoulders. These may have been some kind of support for saggars or trays.

A variety of saggars was discovered, remarkable both in type and size. Many were glazed inside for protecting the wares in the glost kiln, and the majority contained numerous circular holes in the bases and sides, suggesting that Littler was preoccupied with obtaining an efficient circulation of heat. He was possibly influenced by his early training as a salt-glaze potter. One variety of saggar requires special

[1] *The Antique Collector*, Vol. 26, No. 4, August 1955 and *The Connoisseur*, Vol. CXXXVI, No. 548, October 1955.

mention—it is in the form of a cone with an inside diameter at the base of about $4\frac{1}{2}$ inches and a wall thickness of about 1 inch, the inside being unglazed. It is possible that this type was used for biscuit firing of figures, and that the thickness of the saggar wall ensured a slow and even rise of temperature. Another type is also of interest. It consists of a cylindrical container, without top or bottom, of about 12 inches in diameter, glazed on the inside. At the lower end are rectangular holes into which bars of glazed fireclay were cemented to act as supports for flat wares inside.

The rather surprising variation in size which is found in the saggars is also present in the stilts, some of the smallest of which have a diameter of $1\frac{1}{2}$ inches, the largest having a diameter of 7 inches or more. There are four main types, of which the most common can be called the 'knife-edge' type. It consists of a ring of glazed earthenware upon which are fused triangular lengths of fireclay arranged radially. A less common variety has pointed fireclay cones in place of the 'knife-edge' supports fused on to circular, oval or boat-shaped rings. The small circular spur-marks made by these cones are sometimes to be seen on the bases of some Longton porcelain, such as lettuce-leaf sauce-boats, although they are by no means as frequent as the 'knife-edge' stilt-marks. It is interesting to note that Entwistle during his excavations at Liverpool discovered similar stilts of the cone and ring type[1] associated with earthenware wasters in the shraff heap at Chorley Court. Occasionally the Longton 'knife-edge' stilts are formed entirely from one piece of fireclay. An unusual type consists of a ring of refractory clay out of which wedge-shaped pieces have been cut to give a turreted surface for the wares to rest upon. Yet another form of support consists of white clay bobbs of a semi-porcellanous nature, some of which were found fused inside saggars. These bobbs, when intact, should have a central spike.

Although local marl was used for the manufacture of some kiln-furniture, and cheap local coal was readily available, most of the other materials required for making porcelain had to be obtained elsewhere. We have already noted the possibility, in Chapter 2, that the Derbyshire mines may have supplied fine white clay, and contemporary accounts state that clays were imported from Cornwall, Devon, and Dorset. Dr. Pococke in his letters[2] mentions the importation of pipe-clay from Poole for the manufacture of stoneware in the Potteries. It is unfortunate that the records for the supply of ball-clay by the old established firm of Pike Bros. at Poole do not go back beyond July 1791, the date of an agreement between William Pike and various

[1] Now in the possession of Mr. Ernest Allman.
[2] British Museum Add. MS. 15,800.

prominent potters including Josiah Wedgwood, Ralph Baddeley, and John and William Yates. Incidentally Pike married a Staffordshire potter's daughter named Anne Warburton.

Jewitt mentions that Josiah Wedgwood was the prime mover in a petition presented in 1762 for the improvement of transport, and this petition gives a useful picture of existing conditions. It states that clay was brought from Devonshire and Cornwall chiefly to Liverpool, then up the Mersey and Weaver to Winsford in Cheshire, and thence overland to the potteries. An alternative route was the road from the port of Chester. Simeon Shaw also mentions Winsford, and names two men who used horses to carry crates of pottery to Winsford and bring back ball-clay. One of these men sometimes carried 'cream colour' ware on his outward journey to be printed by Sadler and Green at Liverpool.

Mr. Geoffrey Bemrose has allowed me to print the following analysis of prepared but unfired porcelain clay found on the Longton site, and it is interesting to compare this analysis with that of a 'snowman' figure of a heron with a raised wing:[1]

Analyst	Dr. A. T. Green Unfired Clay per cent	Dr. H. W. Webb 'Snowman' figure per cent
Silica	55·53	65·06
Titanic oxide	0·24	0·23
Alumina	3·72	3·60
Ferric oxide	0·79	0·22
Manganese	0·04	—
Lime	13·93	13·54
Magnesia	0·11	0·02
Lead oxide	9·15	10·06
Potash	1·62	2·29
Soda	0·16	0·17
Lithium	0·04	—
Phosphates	2·48	0·80
Sulphates	—	2·98
Loss on ignition	11·92	1·52

In both cases the low alumina and high lead contents, together with the lime percentages, suggest that the glassy paste produced at Longton was composed of ingredients similar to those used at Chelsea during the early 'triangle-mark' period, and also for the 'girl in a swing' group.[2] In the latter class, however, the lead content is usually five to seven per cent higher.

[1] Another example *Plate* 3B.

[2] A distinctive class of figures, possibly of Chelsea origin, produced about 1751.

Simeon Shaw mentions by name a number of Staffordshire potters who were employed at Chelsea from 1747. However, after a short time these workmen left the Chelsea factory to start up a rival concern. Owing to disagreement amongst themselves they abandoned this project and returned to Burslem intending to manufacture china there; but again their plans miscarried, and they took employment in the more profitable salt-glaze industry. It has been suggested that these seceding Chelsea hands produced the 'girl in a swing' specimens.[1] There is the further possibility that William Jenkinson may have obtained his formula for making porcelain from them, perhaps even before they left the Chelsea factory, to which they do not appear to have had any strong allegiance.

The schedule attached to the third agreement lists four different suppliers for large amounts of broken glass, and the use of this ingredient in the paste would account for the high percentage of lead on analysis. Nevertheless, the lead content of Longton porcelain is very variable, even some of the early wares having lead-free analyses.

Furthermore, four different porcelain wasters from the Longton site, including a figure fragment, were all lead-free on testing. Magnesia is another variable constituent; some early Littler's blue-and-white plates contain the merest trace of it, others having levels up to ten per cent. These factors limit the usefulness of chemical analysis, especially in the early, highly experimental period; the prime consideration in every case is a careful study of the paste and glaze and style of potting.

As the excavations proceeded calcined flints were unearthed in appreciable numbers. We know from Dr. Pococke's letters and Shaw's account that flints for 'the Potteries' were obtained from Lincolnshire and other parts, and that they were brought by sea to Liverpool and Hull. From Hull they were shipped up the Trent to Willington and then taken overland to 'the Potteries'. The Longton Hall flint mill has long since disappeared, but a Staffordshire directory for 1851 mentions Gom's Flint Mill, and the lane on the far side of the Longton Brook is still known as Gom's Mill Lane.

Cobalt for the famous 'Littler's blue' may have come from the Derbyshire mines, as English *zaffre* is known to have differed from the finer Saxon product by its deep hue, strongly tinged with indigo, violet, or purple.[2] The best cobalt was a rare and expensive commodity which, according to Ward, was imported from Sweden and Saxony.

[1] W. B. Honey, *English Pottery and Porcelain*, 1933, p. 112.
[2] G. B. Hughes, 'The Development of Cobalt Blue' *Country Life*, Vol. CXV, 3rd June 1954.

Amongst the unexpected finds made during the excavations were a number of fragments of fine salt-glaze, including crabstock handles, coloured pieces with patterns on them, and examples decorated with brilliant cobalt blue. These wasters are proof that Littler manufactured earthenware at Longton, and probably continued to do so as a sideline until the factory's closure in 1760.

The largest piece of porcelain found was a completely collapsed teapot in biscuit with half its lid stuck to the side (1). Its floral moulding is identical with that on two plates in the Rous Lench collection which are decorated with 'Littler's blue' and fine enamel paintings of birds and flower sprays (2). This moulding can also be seen on a *sucrier* in the Victoria and Albert Museum, and on an early teapot in the Fitzwilliam Museum, both decorated with 'Littler's blue'. A few fragments of small double-scroll handles were found, as well as a number of porcelain flowers for fixing to a metal *bocage*.

The two most important finds are now in the Hanley Museum. First, there is a solid tree-trunk base for a white glazed figure of a bird of which only the claws remain. The fragment measures $2\frac{1}{4}$ inches high and has a base of $1\frac{3}{8}$ inches in diameter. It has every appearance of being part of a 'snowman' figure, and there is a typical small central hole in the base as well as two 'snowman' flowers, one in front between a pair of leaves and another applied behind. Second, a more recent discovery is the white glazed figure of a dog, also decorated with 'snowman' flowers. This figure has collapsed in the glost firing, and once formed part of a larger group of which fragments of the base remain. The dog and base fragments are fused on to the bottom of a large cylindrical glazed saggar. Sandwiched between the figure and its container are broken pottery shards which have been used as primitive stilts. The Longton provenance of 'snowman' figures is dealt with more fully in the following chapter.

Towards the end of the factory's life its polychrome version of a Chinese root and fence pattern (3) was produced in some quantity and an example of this decoration has been unearthed. No Longton knife-handles have been recorded previously; but a blue-and-white example was found amongst the wasters, its decoration including a tuft of bent-over rushes, which is a well-recognized Longton peculiarity. Many of the later blue-and-white fragments, matched by examples in specialized collections, confirm that Longton Hall produced a large number of Chinese-influenced blue-and-white patterns.

Both biscuit and glazed wasters of identical shapes and mouldings found on the site prove conclusively that certain types, already attri-

(1) *Plate* 23c; (2) *Plate* 13b; (3) *Plate* 72b.

buted to Longton Hall on other grounds, were in fact made there. Among these types are plates with strawberry mouldings (several large wasters—some unglazed); cream-jugs and other shapes with a particular form of basket moulding (1), represented on the site by fragments of a blue-and-white cream-jug and an unglazed saucer-dish; barrel-shaped teapots with scroll-moulded spouts (fragments included one unglazed spout and several glazed). The definite attribution of these barrel-shaped teapots to Longton is of special importance, as an example in the reserve collection at the British Museum was not decorated at Longton Hall; it bears a rustic transfer design with the signature of Sadler of Liverpool. The same printed design and signature appears on a cream-jug of Longton Hall porcelain in the Cecil Higgins Museum at Bedford (2).

Many more documentary wasters are likely to be unearthed in subsequent excavations at Longton Hall under the cobbled courtyard of the stables. However, enough material is already available, both at the Hanley Museum and in the author's collection, upon which to base a considerable number of definite attributions.

---

(1) *Plate* 70A; (2) *Plate* 76B.

4

EARLY WARES

I have found it convenient to divide the output of the Longton factory into three consecutive periods corresponding with the development of style and technique; but the dividing dates I have chosen are intended only as approximate guides. The first period begins about 1749, when Jenkinson founded the factory on his own account; continues after the first agreement of the 7th of October 1751, when he took partners; and ends with the agreement of the 25th of August 1753, when he relinquished his interest in the factory's affairs. The second or middle period spans the most productive part of the factory's history, from the end of 1753 to October 1757, the month in which the final supplemental agreement was signed. The third period covers less than three years, ending with the final sale at Salisbury in September 1760.

The only newspaper advertisement to appear during the first period was published in *Aris's Birmingham Gazette* on the 27th of July 1752, and was subsequently repeated a number of times. It states that 'a Large Quantity, and great Variety, of very good and fine ornamental Porcelain or China Ware, in the most fashionable and genteel Taste' was for sale by William Littler and Co. at Longton Hall near Newcastle.

In her paper published in 1929[1] Mrs. MacAlister propounded a theory, which has been widely accepted, that the earliest products of the Longton factory were a class of white figures whose blurred modelling, buried under a thick glistening glaze, has earned for them the nickname 'snowmen'. Two 'snowman' figures found on the site of the factory would now seem to confirm the Longton origin of this class, whose many stylistic links with the Staffordshire earthenware and salt-glaze figures had already been noted.

These early Longton figures may be compared, somewhat to their disadvantage, with contemporary figures made in other English porcelain-factories—the so-called 'dry edge' models of Derby,[2] and

[1] *Trans. E.P.C.*, No. 11.
[2] These earliest Derby figures are thought to be modelled by Planché. They often show an unglazed 'dry edge' at the base.

the 'girl in a swing' series[1] made in London. The early Longton modeller appears to have had no special skill, and was evidently hampered by the unresponsive material, of which he can have had no long experience—even if he had previously worked in the unsuccessful Limehouse factory. But in contrast to their primitive execution the 'snowman' class shows a relative sophistication in the range of its subject-matter. Over thirty different models are known, and they suggest familiarity with those made in China, at Meissen, and at Chelsea. It is possible that subjects were suggested by Jenkinson, apparently an educated man with some cultural background.

It seems likely that most of these figures were made about 1750 or possibly slightly earlier, and a small seated pug dog (1) has the date 1750 (which appears to be contemporary) incised in the base. A unique figure of outstanding interest in the Katz Collection shows a mixture of modelling and low relief moulding in the same tradition as early Staffordshire salt-glaze and pottery figures (2). The figure of Fame is reclining on the crest of a wave and beneath her, between two pug dogs, is a gingerbread-like moulding of Bonnie Prince Charlie in highland dress holding a paw of the British lion. Jacobite portrait engraved glasses were popular about 1750, and it is likely that this porcelain representation dates from that time. It is interesting to recall that Prince Charles encamped at Leek in Staffordshire when he invaded England in 1745.

There are Chelsea counterparts of some of the 'snowmen': the group of two recumbent sheep, for example, appears as early as the 'triangle period' (1745-50), with no appreciable difference in size from the Staffordshire model. 'Summer' and 'Winter' (3) were made by both factories, as also the figure of 'Pantaloon'; and it is likely that all these figures derive from Meissen models. There is a rare 'snowman' figure of a seated bagpiper in the Katz Collection, and this model can also be seen on the top of a Bow pot-pourri vase in the Schreiber Collection. It takes its ultimate origin from a sixteenth-century bronze by Giovanni da Bologna. A few of the figures representing birds and deities have a Chinese prototype; one example is a crane taper-holder in the Victoria and Albert Museum after a Fukien model, and another is a *Kuan Yin* which was also copied by Chelsea.

Two unusually elaborate figures (4) are variations on the theme of Cupid at Vulcan's Forge. They are good examples of the incon-

[1] See pp. 22–3.

(1) *Plate* 3c; (2) *Plate* 1; (3) *Plates* 4B *and* C; (4) *Plates* 2A *and* B.

gruous and haphazard decoration with applied rosette-like flowers which is typical of the whole group.

In spite of many adaptations from other sources the outstanding characteristic of 'snowmen' is their obvious kinship with Staffordshire earthenware figures; and it is well known that many of them have lead-glazed or salt-glazed pottery counterparts, especially the standing bagpiper, the recumbent horses, and the large pheasant in the Victoria and Albert Museum. A number were fashioned as taper-holders and candlesticks, as is the case with the turkeycock (1) and hen. Coloured 'snowmen' are extremely rare, but in the Katz Collection there is a figure of 'Summer'; and in the author's collection there is a model of two recumbent sheep, both figures being sparsely decorated with enamels.

As a general rule the hands and feet as well as the faces of 'snowmen' are poorly modelled, and the eyes are represented by simple incised lines. These features are in marked contrast to those found in figures of the other disputed class, known as the 'girl in a swing' group, whose modelling is always fine, and whose porcelain body has a closer and harder texture with a tighter fitting glaze. The Derby 'dry edge' group is also better modelled, the drapery and features being generally crisper and more definite, and the glaze and creamy paste of much finer quality. An interesting white lion (a pair are known in colour) is illustrated by W. B. Honey in his book *Old English Porcelain* and described in the text as probably 'snowman';[1] but the fine modelling, apart from any other consideration, must rule it out of this class. Some 'snowmen' figures, however, are much better modelled than others, and judging by the different styles it seems likely that more than one modeller was employed.

The glaze on 'snowmen' is almost pure glass; it often contains numerous small air-bubbles which give a slight glittering effect and it is usually so thickly applied as to mask the modelling. There appears to have been little cohesion between glaze and paste during the firing, so that glaze-free patches and pools or beads of glaze may occur on the same figure, and where the glaze is very thick, crazing is sometimes present. The undersides of the bases are typically glaze-free, and often show signs of having been brushed or wiped before firing. In these bases is usually a small conical hole, or, more rarely, a somewhat larger one, as in the case of the figure illustrated (2), where it measures three-quarters of an inch in diameter. As a rule the figures are hollow, but they are occasionally solid, as is the fine figure of a heron (3)

[1] *Old English Porcelain*, 1948, Plate 29A.

(1) *Plate* 3A; (2) *Plate* 5A; (3) *Plate* 3B.

B. *Early leaf dish with curled edges. Handle formed as a fruiting fig branch. Shaggy bird decoration. Length 6½ in.*
Dr. and Mrs. Statham Collection
See page 33

preening a raised wing, which probably has a Chinese prototype. The paste of these figures was apparently well protected from the fumes of the kiln, as it is often very white, whereas the earliest useful wares were frequently baked to a yellow colour on their bases and foot rings. It is possible in the former case that the thick conical figure saggars mentioned in Chapter 3 were used to prevent this yellowing effect of coal firing, which Dr. Pococke had noted during his visit to the potteries in 1750, when he stated that the potter from Limehouse could not bake his china 'with coal, which turns it yellow, wood being the fuel which is proper for it'.

Chemical analysis shows that the paste generally contains a measurable percentage of lead, suggesting that flint glass was used in the recipe; but it must be stressed that with such highly experimental figures this percentage as well as that of other ingredients is liable to vary considerably. Chemical analysis has only a limited diagnostic value in such cases.

Fluorescence tests have some confirmatory value, especially with a 'short wave' lamp having a proportionately large output of 2537 Angström Units in conjunction with a Chance OX7 filter of 2 mm. thickness. Under such a lamp the 'snowman' glaze generally 'fluoresces' an intense white, a characteristic reaction which is distinguishable from, although most nearly matched by, the glaze fluorescence of some early French soft paste and that of the 'dry edge' Derby group. Occasionally there is an atypical violet-purple overtone, as shown by the rare 'Lawyer' figure (1). The latter reaction is also given by some glassy Chelsea porcelains of the 'triangle period'. Identical fluorescences can be observed with some early domestic wares, but with others there is a pink overtone to the intense white glaze reaction.

The usual and expected sequence of events in the evolution of an early porcelain factory's history is: first, the production of white wares, then of early underglaze blue-and-white, followed at a slightly later date by overglaze enamel-decorated pieces. The Chelsea factory is one outstanding exception to this rule as it did not produce any quantity of primitive blue-and-white. Complicating factors are that a factory's stock of its earliest white wares was often sent to an outside decorator or was possibly factory-decorated with enamels at a later date after the muffle kilns had been erected. At the Longton factory some of the 'snowmen' figures were without doubt amongst the first products, but the earliest blue-and-white domestic wares are likely to have been contemporary with the majority of these figures because their paste and glaze are practically identical.

(1) *Plate* 5A.

The early domestic pieces are nearly all moulded, the potter's wheel being hardly ever used except for ewers and basins and some tall straight-sided tankards;[1] but the majority of these latter vessels are moulded with floral and scroll reserves based on silver patterns. Basket mouldings were especially favoured, and teapots and coffee pots were commonly of a six-lobed silver shape (1). Others were fluted or moulded with raised borders of flowers, leaves and fruit, in a manner peculiar to Longton. Glazed bases are usual on such objects, but flat unglazed bases occur on mugs and flat ware. Foot rings are frequently ground level, and lids are glazed inside. The 'knife-edge' stilt-marks are broader than those on later wares, and sometimes have fragments of fireclay embedded in them; a typical early 'Littler's blue' mug in the author's collection has seven of these stilt-marks arranged radially on its flat base. Nearly all these wares are thickly potted and heavy in the hand, and judging by their thick, doughy, appearance they plainly represent the first stages in Longton's discovery of the plastic qualities of porcelain clay.

In general the translucency of the early paste is greenish-yellow to cloudy yellow, this depending partly on the degree of firing. Small circular areas of increased translucency known as 'moons' are occasionally present, but these, and the smaller 'flecks', are less common than in the later pastes. Mr. D. A. MacAlister[2] appears to have been the first to draw attention to the fact that 'moons' occurring in porcelain are due to air-bubbles, and not due to aggregations of vitreous frit.

Primitive leaf forms exist in the earliest blue-and-white, and uninhibited painting with Littler's startling ultramarine cobalt sometimes completely covers all but the base of these wares. The strange richness of this ground colour was increased by the lavish use of unfired gold to paint not only borders and outline cartouches on the blue ground, but also sprays of flowers in reserves (2). This unfired gilding has now mostly disappeared, together with any unfired painting which may have been used, leaving the wares with an unfinished appearance (matched by some gold-anchor Chelsea with only mazarine blue decoration). Raised white enamel painted on a background of 'Littler's blue' was a typical but rather unusual form of embellishment which may be seen to advantage on an elaborately painted jug in the Victoria and Albert Museum (3).

---

[1] See the important pair of 'Over Hailes' armorial mugs in the Royal Scottish Museum, Edinburgh, illustrated and described by Mrs. MacAlister, *Trans. E.P.C.*, 1931, No. 111.

[2] *Burlington Magazine*, Vol. LI, October 1927.

---

(1) *Plates 15 and 16*; (2) *Plate 5B*; (3) *Plate 20*.

This type of decoration with an opaque ground underglaze blue, and further ornamentation over the glaze, is likely to be the Longton version of 'japanning'. It will be recalled that japanning is listed with painting, enamelling and gilding in the original agreements, and that there has already been some discussion on this subject in Chapter 2.

Some of the early blue-and-white pieces bear a crossed 'L' mark in blue, frequently with a small tail of dots, up to four in number, underneath. The precise significance of this mark remains obscure although it may have been an attempt to imitate the Vincennes mark.

After the rather garish richness of the early blue-and-white, the coloured wares of the first period are a refreshing change. They are decorated with a surprisingly wide range of pigments in soft and delicate tones. Seven different colours were used for the unusual design on a tall fluted mug (1), and a similar range of enamels is found in the decoration of a six-lobed coffee pot (2) whose blue-and-white counterpart has already been mentioned. The painting on this polychrome coffee pot is particularly fine. It depicts the beautiful little Rose de Meaux, also known as the 'Rose des Peintres', which was one of the first cabbage-roses to be introduced into England. Its small, rather flat blooms, of a light purplish-pink borne on slender stalks, form a more prominent feature of the flower-spray decoration of middle-period wares. The coffee pot's most unusual feature is the child's head knop. This same head appears in a Longton 'mother and child' group formed as a candle-holder. A Bow example of this figure is in the Schreiber Collection.

The very attractive bird-painting of this early period may be seen on a small scalloped-edge plate with a border of 'Littler's blue' (3). It depicts a typical bird and butterfly group reminiscent of the type painted by Charles Fenn, the bird and flower painter, who was living in Battersea in 1753.[1]

Some of the best-potted pieces are decorated with two oriental designs : the quail pattern, and the orange-banded pattern. A teapot (4) with its stand, showing the quail pattern, has a characteristic early spout and handle. An example of the other design on a chamber pot (5) is a free interpretation of the Japanese original. Both designs are known on octagonal teacups and saucers, and the orange-banded pattern also occurs on fluted tea ware.

The figures of Ceres act as connecting links between the 'snowman' class and the early enamelled figures produced towards the end of the early period. The oft-quoted example on the enamelled salt in the

[1] Compare Cyril Cook's *The Life and Work of Robert Hancock*, Item 119.

---

(1) *Plate* 17; (2) *Plate* 15; (3) *Plate* 14; (4) *Plate* 12A; (5) *Plate* 11A.

British Museum (1), and the larger coloured Ceres (2), show the same modelling as their white 'snowman' precursor, with the same broad-backed infant which would hardly have been produced by any other factory. Other figures of this group (3) show that improved technique has permitted a slightly freer posing of the limbs and a better modelling of drapery, though the gestures remain frozen and without rhythm, and the heads give the impression that they are pegged into the shoulders. Nevertheless, in spite of their faults, these rare early figures have an undeniable charm.

---

(1) *Plate* 10A; (2) *Plate* 18C; (3) *Plates* 18A *and* B.

5

THE MIDDLE PERIOD

The four years from 1754 to 1757 are remarkable for the production of a large variety of wares showing greatly improved potting and modelling, as well as possessing considerable aesthetic appeal. In style the figures especially are far in advance of any pottery wares produced in Staffordshire at that time, and they are fully abreast of contemporary developments at Chelsea. This surprising precocity is best seen in the numbers of delightful rococo forms which are the major achievement of the period.

There is, naturally, no abrupt change from the early primitive attempts to the much finer products of the middle period, but during the transitional stage the moulding and modelling continue to improve. The glaze is still very glassy, and the often rather brittle paste is more highly translucent, showing an opalescent green by transmitted light and becoming almost colourless in thinly potted areas.

The Longton powder-blue pieces occur only during this transitional stage, and, although they still exhibit the early paste and glaze, they are painted with a paler, more greyish-blue than that found during the first period. The best known examples are four-sided vases, moulded with the squirrel and grape-vine motif, and decorated with freehand Chinese landscapes similar to those on later blue-and-white wares. Other members of this group are two unusual small vases showing traces of unfired gilding (1), and the rare melon-shaped teapot (2), a model which occurs more often later during the middle period, when it is commonly painted with bright greens and yellows.

A neatly moulded 'silver-shape' sauce-boat (3) has paintings of birds similar to those on Lund's Bristol porcelain. Other birds of the same general type can be seen in the coloured illustration of a delightfully primitive dish (4). Ornamental boxes in the shape of fruits sometimes occur, either separately, or in groups of three fired to stands moulded as grape-vine leaves (5), imitating Meissen originals. A pair of

(1) *Plates* 22A and B; (2) *Plate* 22C; (3) *Plate* 24; (4) *Colour Plate* B; (5) *Plate* 25A.

vases finely decorated in early pigments, including opaque white enamel, show scenes copied from two of Pillement's engravings (1) which later appeared in *The Ladies Amusement*.[1]

An interesting and elaborate teapot (2), similar in shape to one in the Fitzwilliam Museum, has an unusual style of decoration which is occasionally seen on sauce-boats (3) with twig handles and moulded clusters of figs and flowers. Sauce-boats of this type are known with 'Littler's blue' decoration, and polychrome examples were produced in numbers during the transitional stage and later. Their moulding exactly follows that of Meissen pieces. Canister cups with rustic twig and bud handles (4) are decorated in a style reminiscent of salt-glaze with birds, which, both in posture and design of their perches, appear to have been inspired by the engravings of George Edwards (1694-1773). One of the earliest strawberry plates (5) is unusually decorated with birds by another hand—the work of the same artist is seen on a fluted mug (6) belonging to the first period.

The over-elaborate and artless 'Arbour Group' and its two supporting candlesticks (7) repeat two figures of the early period (8), except that the modelling of these somewhat later examples is much improved, especially as regards detail in dress. One of these 'Arbour Groups' can be seen in the Victoria and Albert Museum, but, owing to a technical fault, its glaze is unusually grey. In contrast with this, the figures of a Turk and his companion, from Meissen originals, have a very white appearance. Their modelling is good, except for the face of the Turk's companion, with its incised eyes resembling those of the 'snowman' type. In the past these figures have often been wrongly attributed to Worcester or Derby. The same figures were reproduced at a later date in typical Longton colouring (9), including 'Littler's blue'. Their bases with applied flowers and looped twigs are copied direct from the Meissen examples.

It is possible that the non-phosphatic models of Kitty Clive[2] come within the Longton fold, especially as their paste contains a fair percentage of lead. However, the paste and glaze are atypical on direct inspection, and further evidence is required before any certain attribution can be made.

Chemical analysis alone does not always differentiate between

[1] Second edition, undated, but about 1760, *Plates 43 and 48.*

[2] Kitty Clive, the actress (1711-85) was modelled at Bow in the character of the 'Fine Lady' in Garrick's farce *Lethe.*

(1) *Plate* 21; (2) *Plate* 27A; (3) *Plate* 28A; (4) *Plate* 27B; (5) *Plate* 28B; (6) *Plate* 17; (7) *Plates* 26A, B *and* C; (8) *Plates* 18A *and* B; (9) *Plates* 42 *and* 43.

C. *Figure of cabbage seller. The most outstanding example from the series of Longton market folk. Middle period. Height* $7\frac{3}{4}$ *in.*
Dr. and Mrs. Statham Collection
See page 38

middle-period Longton and contemporary Derby figures, as both may show lead contents in the region of 6 per cent together with the presence or absence of smaller quantities of magnesia and phosphate. In general, however, figures which contain small amounts of phosphate are more likely to be of Longton origin, that substance being uncommon in Derby examples of the same period. Short-wave ultraviolet light gives a somewhat better differentiation, the pink reaction of the Longton glaze contrasting with the bluish-purple fluorescence shown by the glaze on Derby figures.

During the middle period the Longton wares were advertised in the *Manchester Mercury* of the 10th of December 1754, as the first produce of the factory, and in September of the next year the third agreement was made, when Robert Charlesworth became a partner. In the Octobers of 1756 and 1757 the two supplemental agreements were signed as a direct outcome of Charlesworth's continued financial assistance. In between these two agreements the year 1757 was notable for a determined effort to increase trade—a London sale from the 19th to the 25th of April having been previously advertised in the *London Public Advertiser* from the 4th to the 10th and then from the 12th to the 25th of that month. In June of the same year an important advertisement appeared in the *Birmingham Gazette*, and both this and the London advertisement now listed useful items together with the more ornamental wares—white and enamelled china and blue-and-white tea-services being mentioned, as well as melons and cauliflowers, 'elegant epergnes' and figures and flower ornaments for dessert.

The best products of the middle period have an attractive elegance which was never attained earlier. There is an emphasis on leaf and fruit forms, which are often painted with a fresh yellowish-green; their light and crisp quality is partly due to the character of the paste and glaze, and partly to the skill of the modelling. Some of the most charming objects are moulded with strawberry leaves, ranging from the more usual plates (1) and dishes to the rare and delicate cream-jugs with green intertwined handles (2). Large water-jugs with this leaf motif have unusually elaborate features, such as whole auricula plants in full bloom, moulded on their sides (3). Beautifully moulded peach cups (4), leaf basins and stands (5), and fragile openwork pieces (6) are among the finest wares ever produced in English soft paste.

The most outstanding characteristic is the charm and lyrical nature of Longton's rococo figures, which are, without doubt, an original

(1) *Plate* 46A; (2) *Plate* 54B; (3) *Plate* 49B; (4) *Plate* 67A; (5) *Plate* 58A; (6) *Plates* 38A *and* 39.

contribution to English ceramics. The finest examples show a perfect blend of abstract composition and representational form; many have a spiral motif with their bases forming an integral part of the composition and echoing the main theme. The group of fruit-sellers and other figures in the late Lord Fisher's collection[1] show this type of construction to advantage.

From the middle period onwards gold was used frequently but rather sparingly on figures, and, in contrast to the earlier practice, only very occasionally on the domestic wares. The early granular dull gilding now gives place to gilding having a more brassy appearance, which is much less attractive. This later gilding has been properly fired and burnished, and was used to pick out buttons and ornaments on the dress and to emphasize the scrollwork on the bases of figures.

The Longton factory produced a very great variety of shapes and forms in its domestic and ornamental wares during this short time-span, and although the polychrome designs of the middle period are somewhat limited, there is a predominance of flower spray painting by the 'Trembly Rose' painter and his copyists, so called because of a fondness for thin cotton-like stems and crinkled petals.

The uniformity of decoration suggests that very little Longton porcelain was decorated outside the factory, although we know from his account-book that Duesbury decorated Staffordshire figures, probably both salt-glaze and porcelain, when he was working in London between 1751 and 1753. In 1754 Duesbury apparently moved to Longton Hall, and Bemrose records that a child of his was baptized at Longton in October of that year. Jewitt stated that he had in his possession two agreements, one dated the 27th of September 1755, referring to Duesbury as being 'of Longton Hall', and the other dated the 1st of January 1756, describing him as of 'Longton in ye County of Stafford, Enameller'.[2] In the schedule attached to the Longton third agreement Mr. Duesbury's name is listed as if he were working at the factory. It is likely that he enamelled figures there for Littler as he was living at Longton for two years before he moved to Derby in 1756.

It is highly probable that John Hayfield, who was described in the third agreement, dated 1755, as the only painter employed at the factory at that time, is none other than the 'Castle Painter', a number of whose attractive continental scenes appear on teapots (1) and other wares. Fine examples are known on dishes moulded with hollyhock

---

[1] J. L. Dixon, *English Porcelain of the Eighteenth Century*, Plate 67.
[2] Both agreements are now in the Victoria and Albert Museum.

(1) *Plate* 71A.

leaves (1), and an unusual European figure painting of his is to be seen on a spoon tray (2).

Black linear pencilling is a rare form of ornamentation; it appears on some beautifully moulded sauce-boats (3), which have salt-glaze and Derby equivalents, and is occasionally seen on small dishes with fluted edges of the same shape as a blue-and-white version (4). One of these pencilled dishes bears the rare impressed cross mark.

Bird-painting is particularly attractive, especially when it occurs on fluted cups and saucers. A fine openwork stand with this form of decoration is in the Seattle Museum (5). This painting is sometimes considered to have been done by James Giles at his enamelling works in Kentish Town; but a direct comparison with the 'Trembly Rose' flower painting shows that the same palette was used in both cases.

Pigments are much brighter than those used earlier, but the colour-scheme is rather unbalanced compared with the earlier palette, because of the predominance of a bright purplish-pink. Other favourite pigments are an orange-red, an opaque greenish-yellow and opaque blue, a bluish- and a yellowish-green. A thick red-brown colour is sometimes used, especially on figures. Eyebrows are usually painted in black, with a black pupil in the centre of a red iris, having two red lines above the eye for the lashes, exactly as with some Meissen examples, and the cheeks are frequently heavily tinted with red pigment.

It is difficult to date the Longton pug dogs (6), copied from the Meissen *Mops*, with their underglaze manganese decoration, and also the rare cow-shaped cream-jugs which are decorated in the same manner. In Mr. Ernest Allman's collection is the only example of the latter known to be complete, having a lid moulded with a honey-bee in the same manner as some silver models (7). Their glaze is unusually greyish, and under short-wave ultra-violet light it gives a marked purplish-pink fluorescence instead of the usual pink reaction. Some of the pug dogs are marked with the crossed 'L' mark painted underglaze in blue in a much bolder fashion than is usual on the early wares. All the marked pug dogs I have seen are decorated with early gilding on the collars and bases; there are examples in the late Lord Fisher's collection, in the Hanley Museum, and in the collection of Mr. Ernest Allman.

A group of interesting primitive figures have rather bloated and flattened faces, the best example being a fine model of a musician (8), copied from Meissen, which expresses the spirit of music as well as

---

(1) *Plate* 36A; (2) *Plate* 65A; (3) *Plate* 47B; (4) *Plate* 71C; (5) *Plate* 39; (6) *Plate* 35A; (7) *Plate* 35B; (8) *Plate* 29A.

if not better than, the more technically perfect hard-paste original. A less satisfactory figure is a crudely modelled flautist (1) also from a Meissen source. A complete series of Seasons (2) in the Fitzwilliam Museum show the same facial characteristics, as does the unusual fruit-seller (3) decorated with fantastically large roses and leaves arranged in such a way as to make quite a satisfactory composition. This type of flower-decoration is seen on the bases of the two cooks (4), models which were adapted at Plymouth for their well-known musicians. The pair of figures with beady eyes and holding flowering sprays, copied at Derby somewhat later, have obviously been produced by the modeller of the 'Arbour Group' (5). The strange infant-Hercules type of child seen in the Ceres figure is now modelled on horseback with a baying hound running beside him (6)

Columbine and Harlequin (7) are well known both in their Meissen originals, and in the soft-paste versions from English factories; but nowhere were they more charmingly portrayed than at Longton. The reading figures form another attractive series whose finest example is a male figure wearing a coat decorated with a soft pink contrasting with his black hat (8). The more flamboyant figures of the flower-seller (9) and the cabbage-seller, the latter here illustrated in colour (10), are two of the finest examples that this period produced, and the stolid countrywoman is a complete contrast to her dandy companion. The modelling is less fussy than that of the figures of a gallant and his lady playing with dogs (11).

The Plymouth factory later produced hard-paste versions of the Putti feeding a goat with flowers or grapes, representing two of the 'Seasons'. The Longton examples are frequently decorated with the rather darker mid-period version of Littler's underglaze blue (12). A much rarer figure of an infant painter with a palette (13) is possibly from a set of 'The Arts', but no other figures from the series are recorded.

Separate porcelain stands were occasionally made for figures, and two examples of Hercules slaying the Nemean lion (14) are known mounted in this way. Two rare 'Scops owls' in the Schreiber Collection are also provided with stands of a similar type.[1]

The highly elaborate pot-pourri vase, here illustrated in colour (15),

[1] Schreiber Collection, Victoria and Albert Museum, No. 150. Catalogued as Chelsea, but considered by the present author to be of Longton origin.

---

(1) *Plate* 29B; (2) *Plates* 30A, B, C *and* D; (3) *Plate* 31A; (4) *Plates* 57B *and* C; (5) *Plates* 34B *and* C; (6) *Plate* 31B; (7) *Plates* 40A *and* B; (8) *Plate* 45B; (9) *Plate* 61C; (10) *Colour Plate* C; (11) *Plates* 67B *and* 68B; (12) *Plate* 64A; (13) *Plate* 51; (14) *Plate* 59A; (15) *Colour Plate* D.

is a technical *tour de force* with its masses of applied flowers and birds. This vase is useful as a reference piece, and its ornaments can be matched with other specimens—such as the flowers decorating the *bocages* of an important pair of elongated figures of 'Lovers with a bird cage' (1), wearing fancy dress as pilgrims, with scallop shells on their capes after the symbol of the Order of St. James of Compostella. Even the figure of a girl on the vase cover has its counterpart in a separate, rather coquettish, dancing figure (2). Bird figures are rather uncommon, and, apart from the owls already referred to, they usually form parts of larger pieces such as candlesticks (3) and ornamental melons (4). Occasionally they occur as brightly-coloured knops on vase covers, and we have already seen that it is possible for the large 'prickly' pot-pourri vases to have a whole medley of birds on them. The pigeon tureens (5), with the male pigeon slightly larger than the female, are amongst Longton's most satisfactory models. Porcelain fruits and vegetables were mentioned in the firm's advertisements, and were produced in a wide variety, including peaches, lemons, melons, cauliflowers and cabbages.

The paste of the middle period as shown by transmitted light is predominantly an opalescent green, which may occasionally have a white, yellow, or blue element in it. The opalescence has a waxy quality and there are frequent small air-bubbles as well as tears in the paste, giving the impression af light flecks. Some of these can be seen on direct inspection as they lie on the surface of the paste under the glaze. In the thicker wares, such as the strawberry leaf-dishes and plates, larger air-bubbles appear as 'moons'. The glaze is soft, and has a silky feeling suggesting a high content of lead. It is much more thinly applied than that on the early wares, and is sometimes slightly opaque, although usually colourless or somewhat greyish. A line of scum is frequently seen near the bases of domestic wares, and long thin stilt-marks with embedded fireclay are common on the undersides. Circular footrings of cups and saucers are often of a squat, triangular section, whereas those of hexagonal shapes have a broad rectangular section. Cups are usually rather tall and narrow; their handles are typically of the double-scroll type, though occasionally ear-shaped and formed from a simple roll of clay. Twin bands of basket moulding are seen on a variety of wares, including a sauce boat with an unusual drip-catcher below the lip (6). Tea-services were produced with this moulding, painted with a yellow ground, and finely decorated with exotic birds in the reserved panels.

(1) *Plates* 66B *and* C; (2) *Plate* 56A; (3) *Plate* 44A; (4) *Plate* 44B; (5) *Plate* 59B; (6) *Plate* 70B.

Blue-and-white patterns were generally derived from Chinese porcelain, and were often painted in a rapid freehand manner, as for example on the cup and saucer here illustrated (1), which bears the same decoration as that on a large two handled cup in the Hanley Museum. The so called 'Folly' pattern (2) was executed with more care, as were the designs on the somewhat earlier octagonal cups and saucers (3). From the numbers still surviving it appears that at least forty blue-and-white patterns were produced, of which the author possesses examples of over thirty. Some are marked with workmen's marks in the form of letters of the alphabet, and others with numerals.

Teapots were produced in a remarkable variety of shapes,[1] many of which, like the important tulip teapot (4), suggest the influence of Meissen porcelain. A large Longton bowl and cream-jug of this unusual pattern are in the Victoria and Albert Museum. The green rustic handle of the teapot is continued downwards to encircle the base and to form the footring, and is then prolonged upwards and enlarged to form the spout. The pineapple teapot (5) is a startling creation which has a mellower pottery counterpart. Another teapot finely decorated by the 'Castle Painter' (6) has been spoilt by an absurdly rustic spout. Acorn knobs were popular, especially on the more simple barrel-shaped teapots which were produced in quantity towards the end of the factory's life.

Apart from widespread Meissen influences—common to all English porcelain at that time—a number of Longton ornamental and domestic pieces of the middle period show a strong Chelsea influence, and from the illustration alone the simple polychrome cup and saucer here shown (7) could easily be mistaken for 'red anchor' pieces. However, the Longton factory only rarely attained the technical perfection achieved by their more successful and senior competitor. Even in spite of an improvement in potting methods technical faults were nearly always present. Nowadays, of course, these faults do not necessarily detract from the appeal of the pieces : they may even, at times, enhance it.

[1] *The Antique Collector*, Vol. 26, No. 1, February 1955.

(1) *Plate* 69A; (2) *Plate* 64B; (3) *Plate* 48A; (4) *Plate* 41B; (5) *Plate* 54A; (6) *Plate* 49A; (7) *Plate* 58B.

D. *A very elaborate pot-pourri vase and cover*
Middle period. Height 16 in.
Mrs. J. Smith Collection
See page 38

6

LATE WARES

During the period of less than three years ending with the final sale at Salisbury from market day the 16th to market day the 20th of September 1760, William Littler made a last desperate effort to establish the Longton factory as a profitable concern. He concentrated mainly on the production of useful wares, and an advertisement in the *Birmingham Gazette* for the 12th of June 1758 lays emphasis on services, especially blue-and-white, rather than single pieces. A London warehouse was opened, but probably owing to competition from Chelsea and Bow it was closed less than a year later; an advertisement in the *London General Evening Post* dated the 30th of September to the 3rd of October 1758 announces the opening of this warehouse in St. Paul's Churchyard. Blue-and-white is again listed before enamelled wares; and coffee, tea and chocolate equipages are given prominence over 'curious parfume pots, vauses, figures and flowers'.

In spite of this policy to produce large quantities of useful wares Littler did not neglect figure-modelling; realizing, as he must have done, that figures were the factory's finest and most individual achievement, he spared no effort to increase their importance and make them more desirable. Large monumental forms were evolved, imbued with a new seriousness and often depicting personalities or themes of current interest.

Simpler forms were favoured for domestic wares. Barrel-shaped teapots, for example, were produced in greater numbers; as were tall, straight-sided cylindrical mugs with double scroll handles. The handsome bell-shaped mugs were not quite so common. Polychrome designs tended to be painted without much care, as if quantity rather than quality was the aim. Chinese patterns were common, such as the root-and-hedge pattern (1), best shown on a somewhat earlier beautiful bowl (2) which is now the envied possession of Mrs. Harnan in America.

Many of the mugs and some of the barrel-shaped teapots were,

(1) *Plate* 72B; (2) *Plate* 60B.

until recently, thought to be of Liverpool origin because they are decorated with transfer prints by Sadler of Liverpool,[1] the majority of these prints being signed.

A natural assumption would be that the Longton factory sent goods direct to Sadler for printing and return. But it appears that it was Sadler's early practice to buy outright the plain goods he intended to decorate. He did this, for example, with Wedgwood's cream ware from 1761 to 1763—the arrangement in this case being that Wedgwood should subsequently buy back as many of the transfer-decorated pieces as he needed. In 1763 a new arrangement came into force whereby Wedgwood's cream wares remained his property throughout, and Sadler charged him for the printing only. In the same year Sadler wrote to Wedgwood stating that he had never printed a piece for any other person; meaning, presumably, that he had not previously worked on commission for any of the other manufacturers. It is even probable that he did not usually buy his white wares direct from the factories. He mentions in another letter dated 1763 buying undecorated wares from a 'Mr. Statham and the rest', who appear to have acted as intermediaries.

Contemporary accounts and advertisements make it clear that Staffordshire pottery was frequently sold to the trade, then mainly travelling 'pot carriers' or 'packmen'. These middlemen are likely to have bought wares in the white from the Longton factory for re-sale to Sadler, to be decorated by his quick and inexpensive method of transfer-printing at Liverpool; a port which was in any case one of the major centres of distribution for Staffordshire wares.

An examination of existing pieces seems to indicate that the Liverpool porcelain-makers were producing surprisingly few well-potted mugs suitable for overglaze printing between the years 1757 and 1760, Chaffers's factory being the exception. Consequently the Longton porcelain mugs should have found a ready market in Liverpool, especially when one considers that they must have been available at highly competitive prices for some little time before the Longton factory closed down.

In August 1763, Sadler wrote to Wedgwood that he had neither quart- nor pint-size copper-plates of the King of Prussia, nor any at all of Wolfe, and asked if he should get them engraved. It might appear from this that the Longton mugs transfer-printed with these designs were decorated in or after 1763. But this was not necessarily the case,

[1] W. Moss in *The Liverpool Guide* 1799 claims that Messrs. Sadler and Green began to print on China and earthenware as early as 1752. However, it is generally believed that transfer printing on ceramics originated at Battersea about 1753 and that Sadler did not use this method of decoration at Liverpool until two or three years later.

as we are led to believe that Sadler arranged for an entirely new set of plates to be engraved for Wedgwood's business.[1] Sadler himself was a printer and not an engraver, and it is possible that some of the early King of Prussia and Wolfe plates remained the property of the engraver and were not available in 1763. Another possibility is that the earlier plates, which would have been in great demand from 1759 to 1760, had become worn and required re-engraving.

It is clear, however, that some Longton porcelain, for example the George III coronation mug, was decorated by Sadler a few months after the factory had closed down, although most of the other wares were probably decorated in the last year of the existence of the Longton factory.

Many of the signed transfers commemorate the heroes of the Seven Years' War (1756-63), and others depict the Arms of societies such as the 'Society of Bucks' and the 'Foresters'. Transfers of Coats of Arms belonging to individuals are unusual; but Dr. Knowles Boney possesses an example bearing the crest of the FitzSteven family (1), and the Manx Museum has a pair of mugs with the Coat of Arms of Mark Hildersley (2) who was Bishop of Sodor and Man from 1755 until his death in 1772. Dr. Boney also owns a bell-shaped mug on which is a distinguished transfer copied from an engraving, after a painting by Philip Mercier, depicting Bonnie Prince Charlie in armour wearing the Ribbon of the Garter (3). Under his portrait are the words 'Ab obice major', a Jacobite motto meaning 'Greater because of the opposition'.

In 1758 the Derby factory announced that owing to the great demand for their goods they had doubled their number of hands. Any suggestion that these new workmen came from Longton Hall is discounted by the fact that the Longton factory was producing sufficient porcelain in the same year to enable them to open a London warehouse. However, as a result of stylistic comparisons, it is practically certain that, after the close of the Longton factory, at least one of its best figure modellers was taken on at Derby; this was the modeller of 'The Musicians' (4) and 'The Dancers' (5) (sometimes described as 'The Lovers'), which are considered by many to be the best-formed of all Longton figures.[2] All these figures are exceptionally tall, and are likely to have been Longton's first attempt at large-scale pieces. They stand on bases reminiscent of those of the figures of the 'Lovers with a bird cage' (6), and it is probable that the same modeller was re-

[1] E. Stanley Price, *John Sadler*, 1950, p. 26.
[2] William King in *English Porcelain Figures of the 18th Century*, 1925, actually attributes these figures to Derby.

(1) *Plate* 79A; (2) *Plate* 79C; (3) *Plate* 79B; (4) *Plates* 74A *and* B; (5) *Plate* 73; (6) *Plates* 66B *and* C.

sponsible for all of them. An undecorated example of 'The Dancers' is in the Fitzwilliam Museum, as are also the late Lord Fisher's coloured 'Dancers' together with his pair of 'Musicians'. The coloured figures are decorated with the usual purples, yellows and greens in addition to the opaque red-brown pigment and good quality gilding. Lord Fisher's examples have been tested and found to be slightly phosphatic, a finding in keeping with their Longton origin. In the Wallace Elliott collection there was an undecorated salt-glaze pair of 'The Musicians' which may have been made at Longton Hall. Two earlier Longton figures, the Turk and his companion, are also believed to have been produced in salt-glaze[1] as well as porcelain (1) at the Longton factory.

The largest figure attributed to Longton is in the Statham Collection. It depicts a sea-god, possibly representing one of a set of 'Elements', wearing a crown formed from ships' prows. It stands $16\frac{1}{2}$ inches high and is well modelled but undecorated. Its attribution to Longton awaits further confirmation.

On a smaller scale the figure of Minerva (2) has simplicity and strength not seen in the various other English models of this figure. Its less attractive Plymouth version is illustrated in the catalogue of the Trapnell Collection. The impressive figure of David Garrick (1717-79), of which there are examples in Lord Fisher's collection and at South Kensington, is in the same tradition as the 'Minerva' and both are mounted on plain rectangular bases. The Longton factory produced an exceedingly rare set of 'Seasons' in a more lyrical mood; only 'Winter' (3) of this set is known to me, although a number of Plymouth versions of all four of them survive.

The Longton figure modellers were evidently proud of their ability to model horses, and in the middle period they had already produced a fine pair led by a Turk (4) and a Blackamoor (5), which were almost exact replicas of Meissen originals. Then, in the last year of the factory's existence, they produced their masterpiece, which depicts the Duke of Brunswick trampling upon French trophies on his prancing steed (6). In this figure the Meissen influence has been well digested; it bears the stamp of originality, and suggests the liveliness of action. The rather wistful Duke is wearing the Order of the Garter, with which he was invested on the 16th of August 1759, after the Battle of Minden. This dates the figure with fair accuracy. The large 'Britannia' model holding a portrait medallion of George II (7)

[1] The Schreiber Collection, nos. 173 and 174, Victoria and Albert Museum.

(1) *Plates* 42 *and* 43; (2) *Plate* 78; (3) *Plate* 75; (4) *Plate* 63C; (5) *Plate* 63B; (6) *Colour Plate* A; (7) *Plate* 77.

sometimes found on a separate three-cornered stand. These stands are decorated with transfers, which have been somewhat crudely enamelled, representing rather elaborate scenes from the Seven Years' War. Both the 'Britannia' illustrated, and an example which Mr. Charles Staal recently purchased in Holland, are unusually decorated on the figures with typical Liverpool two- or three-colour outline transfers and superadded enamels.

Amongst the last figures produced at Longton were the 'Four Continents' (1), and in them the factory achieved its most mature expression—'Europe' being perhaps the finest of the four. Mr. Cavendish has kindly permitted me to quote the chemical analysis of his undecorated figure of 'Asia':

Silica	62·0 per cent
Lead Oxide	10·0 per cent
Alumina and Iron	6·0 per cent
Lime	17·5 per cent
Phosphate	0·6 per cent
Magnesia	0·2 per cent
Soda	1·3 per cent
Potash	2·4 per cent

It will be noted that this analysis comes fairly near that of the Longton transfer-printed mug recorded by Eccles and Rackham.[1] Both analyses resemble those of a number of the earliest Longton wares which have a similar percentage of lead and lime in the paste. This would seem to indicate that in spite of intervening experiments with different quantities of lead, lime, magnesia and phosphate, the original recipe was used with little variation for some at least of the late wares. Chipped or broken parts of these late figures frequently show brown or black specks of impurities in the paste, suggesting lack of care in the preparation of the clay. By transmitted light the paste often has a dirty brown colour which is quite distinct from the green translucency of the useful wares of the same period. Another distinctive feature is the white fluorescence of their glaze under short-wave ultra-violet light, which contrasts with the dark pink fluorescence of the later table wares.

The 'Continents' were later produced from the same or similar moulds at Plymouth. The Longton soft-paste examples are immediately distinguishable from the Plymouth hard-paste versions by the flat undersides of their bases, the Plymouth figures being com-

[1] *Analysed Specimens of English Porcelain* (No. 9).

(1) *Plates* 80A *to* D.

pletely hollow underneath. Moreover, the Longton examples are better modelled and tend to be somewhat more elaborate, having a number of applied flowers and leaves, especially on the figures of 'Asia' and 'America'. Other differences exist, the most noticeable being that in the Longton 'Africa' an elephant mask is held in the figure's right hand, whereas in the Plymouth model the mask lies between her feet. The complete set at Temple Newsam is illustrated here for the first time, but in the catalogue of the Trapnell Collection another set of Longton 'Continents' is shown as Plymouth, and Severne Mackenna makes the same error in describing and illustrating some of Mr. Stephen Simpson's 'Continents' in his monograph on Cookworthy's porcelain.[1]

It is remarkable that nearly all Plymouth figures show a strong Staffordshire influence, the majority having Longton counterparts, but it seems an improbable explanation of this fact that William Cookworthy bought the complicated moulds, or even the disarticulated master-figures, at the Salisbury sale eight years before he founded his own factory; and further there is no mention of factory furniture in the sale's printed advertisement. It is more likely that the original models of the Longton set of 'Continents' and of other figures had been retained by an independent artist, and that new moulds were later cast from them at Plymouth, the Longton factory having ceased to hold any rights over them after it had failed. The existence of one independent artist modeller is revealed by Champion's correspondence concerning the Bristol hard paste set of 'Elements' which he commissioned from an artist who also produced models for Derby.

* * * * *

The Longton factory was still in production when Robert Charlesworth published his announcement of the dissolution of the partnership from the 23rd of May 1760, which appeared in *Aris's Birmingham Gazette* on the 9th of June of that year. In it he mentioned that Mr. Samuel Boyer, an attorney living at Newcastle-under-Lyme, had full power and authority to recover, as his Agent, any debts owing to the Company. Three weeks later, on the 30th of June, the same paper printed William Littler's reply, stating that 'it's not in Robert Charlesworth's Power to dissolve the Partnership therein mentioned, without Consent of the rest of the Partners; that the said William Littler and Co. are far from the Expectation of any Credit on the said Charlesworth's Account and are all very desirous to execute any proper Instrument for the Dissolution of the said Partnership, on

[1] *Cookworthy's Plymouth and Bristol Porcelain* 1946, *Figures* 91c, 92c *and* 94c.

having fair Accounts settled, and Damages paid by the said Charles-worth for his many Breaches of Covenant, and his late unjustifiable and illegal, tho' impotent and ineffectual, Attempt to put a Stop to the said Manufactory: And as the said Littler and Co. are a Majority of the said Partners, and have, by Articles of Partnership, not only an un-doubted Right of disposing of the Partnership Effects, but in all Matters of Moment their Decision is final; therefore they give Notice to all Persons not to deliver any of the Goods or Effects belonging to the said Partnership to the said Robert Charlesworth, or either of them: And that all Gentlemen, Ladies, and others, may be fitted at Longton aforesaid, with much better Wares than ever, at reasonable Rates, by William Littler and Co.'.

Littler meant what he said, and was doubtless prepared to continue the work for the rest of the term of fourteen years; but, even before the *Birmingham Gazette* could publish Samuel Firmin's confirmation of Charlesworth's announcement, the whole stock from the factory had been seized out of Littler's grasp by Charlesworth's agents and taken to Salisbury for the final sale. It is not absolutely clear why Salisbury should have been chosen. The city was, however, an im-portant and prosperous centre in those days, mostly on account of the wool trade. Furthermore, the London market had already been tried unsuccessfully and the Midlands were flooded with porcelain from Derby and elsewhere. Salisbury is near Poole, and, as water transport was considerably cheaper than road transport in the eighteenth cen-tury,[1] it is probable that the factory's stock was taken in the reverse direction over the well-established route for ball clay—coastwise via Liverpool or Chester to Poole, and then possibly, either overland, or by barge up the Wiltshire Avon, which appears to have been at least partly navigable in those days.

The sale was conducted by an exchange broker from Cheapside in London, and its announcement in the *Salisbury Journal* dated the 8th of September 1760, reviews the major part of the factory's output during the middle and late periods. It consisted of 'upwards of ninety thousand Pieces of the greatest variety of Dresden Patterns, in rich enamel'd, pencil'd, Blues and Gold; as Figures and Flowers, mounted in Chandeliers, Essence Jars, Beakers, Vases, and Perfume Pots, magnificent Dessert Services; Sets of Bowls, Mugs, Dishes and Plates, ornamented with Columbines and Central Groups; Tea, Coffee and Toilet Equipages, of elegant Patterns, superbly furnish'd, equal to a National Factory, so eminently distinguish'd, with a profusion of use-ful and ornamental Articles'.

It is likely that most of the stock went in large lots to the trade and

[1] W. T. Jackman, *Transportation in Modern England*, Vol. 1, 1916.

was widely dispersed, but some local relics of the sale have been traced, for not long before the last World War a London dealer found a strawberry plate used for displaying jujubes in a Salisbury sweet shop, and Dr. Statham told me that he once bought a whole leaf-moulded service for less than fifty pounds at a private sale within the boundaries of the same city.

Longton Hall was the first porcelain factory in Staffordshire. During the short life-span of ten years it was, from start to finish, a highly speculative concern, and a certain unevenness in quality of its productions was doubtless due to insufficient finance. Its enterprising manager, William Littler, had perhaps aimed too high in his endeavour to compete with foreign state-sponsored factories, but his achievement was nonetheless very considerable. Both he and William Jenkinson had broken away from the traditional conservatism of the potteries in producing their glassy wares; but their lack of financial success appears to have had an inhibitory effect for some time afterwards on porcelain production in Staffordshire, and it was more than twenty years before any large quantity was made there again.

After the factory's failure we hear no more of William Littler, except for Shaw's uncorroborated statement that he became the manager of the firm of Baddeley and Fletcher. If he did so, it appears that his spirit had been crushed; for there remains to us nothing that shows the same originality of conception, or the same striving for perfection, which had been his achievement and his ambition at Longton Hall.

MARKS

The crossed 'L' mark, with or without a short tail of dots beneath it, occurs in underglaze blue on some early pieces which have 'Littler's blue' as part of their decoration. It is also known in gilt on a unique blue-and-white sugar caster in Mr. W. L. Little's collection. Pug dogs decorated with underglaze manganese blotches occasionally bear the crossed 'L' mark usually broadly painted in underglaze blue. It may be an imitation of the Vincennes mark; but the two letters often appear as a 'J' crossed with an 'L', possibly representing Jenkinson, Longton.

Sometimes other cross forms occur:

in underglaze
blue.

incised marks.

Other incised marks occur mostly on coloured, leaf-shaped wares of the middle period:

    ⊙   the sign for gold

    ⊖   the sign for salt

    ♀   the sign for copper

    ☿   the sign for mercury

Various letters of the alphabet or numerals are found in underglaze blue as workmen's marks on middle and late period blue-and-white wares.

BIBLIOGRAPHY

R. PLOT, *The Natural History of Staffordshire*, 1686.

DR. R. POCOCKE, *Tours*. British Museum Additional MS. 15,800. 1750.

REV. STEBBING SHAW, *The History of the County of Stafford*. 1798.

W. PITT, *Topographical History of Staffordshire*. 1817.

SIMEON SHAW, *History of the Staffordshire Potteries*. 1829.

J. WARD, *History of the Borough of Stoke-upon-Trent*. 1843.

REV. T. HARWOOD, *Survey of Staffordshire*. 1844.

W. EVANS, *The Art and History of the Pottery Business*. 1846.

E. METEYARD. *The Life of Josiah Wedgwood* (2 vols.). 1865.

L. JEWITT, *The Wedgwoods: being a life of Josiah Wedgwood*. 1865.

J. HASLEM, *The Old Derby China Factory*. 1876.

L. JEWITT, *The Ceramic Art of Great Britain* (2 vols.). 1878.

J. E. NIGHTINGALE, *Contributions Towards the History of Early English Porcelain From Contemporary Sources*. Salisbury, 1881.

F. RATHBONE, *Old Wedgwood*. B. Quaritch, 1893.

W. BEMROSE, *Bow, Chelsea and Derby Porcelain*. Bemrose & Sons, 1898.

W. BEMROSE, *Longton Hall Porcelain*. Bemrose & Sons, 1906.

G. W. RHEAD, *Staffordshire Pots and Potters*. Hutchinson & Co., 1906.

The Trapnell Collection of Bristol and Plymouth Porcelain. 1912.

J. C. WEDGWOOD, *Staffordshire Pottery and its History*. 1913.

H. ECCLES and B. RACKHAM, *Analysed Specimens of English Porcelain*. London, South Kensington Museum, 1922.

B. RACKHAM, *Catalogue of the Schreiber Collection, in the Victoria and Albert Museum* (vol. 1, second edition). 1928.

R. NICHOLLS, *Ten Generations of a Potting Family*. P. Lund Humphries & Co., 1928.

English Porcelain Circle Transactions. 1928-32.

English Ceramic Circle Transactions. 1933-51.

MRS. D. MACALISTER, *William Duesbury's London Account Book 1751-1753*. 1931.

B. RACKHAM, *Catalogue of the Glaisher Collection*. 1934.

S. MACKENNA, *Cookworthy's Plymouth and Bristol Porcelain*. 1946.

English Ceramic Circle Exhibition Catalogue. 1948.

W. B. HONEY, *Old English Porcelain* (second edition). Faber and Faber, 1948.

BIBLIOGRAPHY

(*Magazine Articles*)

W. B. HONEY, *English Pottery and Porcelain* (fourth edition). A. and C. Black, 1949.

E. S. PRICE, *John Sadler*. 1950.

MRS. W. HODGSON, *The Connoisseur*, Vol. XIII, December 1905.

NORAH RICHARDSON, *The Connoisseur*, Vol. XXXIV, December 1912.

MRS. D. MACALISTER, *Apollo*, Vol. V, January 1927, and Vol. X, November-December 1929.

W. B. HONEY, *Old Furniture*, Vol. III, February 1928.

B. M. WATNEY, *The Antique Collector*, Vol. 26, No. 1, February 1955; No. 2, April 1955; No. 4, August 1955.

B. M. WATNEY, *The Connoisseur*, Vol. CXXXVI, October 1955.

Appendix A
THE LONGTON HALL AGREEMENTS

The original agreements are lengthy legal documents containing a certain amount of repetition. The author has taken the liberty of extracting and condensing only the relevant details.

The First Agreement, dated the 7th of October 1751

Our only knowledge of this agreement is contained in the following references to it in the second agreement. It was 'Made or Mentioned to be made between the said William Jenkinson of the First part the said William Nicklin of the Second part and the said William Littler of the Third part Thereby Reciteing that the said William Jenkinson had Obtained the Art Secret or Mystery of making a Certain porcelain Ware in Imitation of China Ware And was then Carrying on a work for making the Same and for the Considerations in the said Indenture Mentioned Agreed to take the said William Nicklin and William Littler partners therein for the Term of Fourteen years from the day of the Date of the said Indenture and the said Work to be Divided into Twelve Equal parts or Shares Five of which said Shares were to be the property of and belong to the said William Jenkinson Other Five of the said Shares to be the property of and belong to the said William Nicklin and the Remaining other Two of these Shares to be the property of and belong to the said William Littler together with the like Shares of all Tools Modells Moulds Mills and Other Utensils and also of Certain Household Goods purchased from Obadiah Lane Esquire (and Contained in a Schedule to the said Indenture Annexed) And of the Term and Interest of the said William Jenkinson in a Lease from the said Obadiah Lane of Longton Hall and the Buildings and premises therewith Demised And Also of All porcelain Ware then Made or in Making And of the said Indenture It is therefore Witnessed that the said parties for the Considerations herein Mentioned Did Mutually Covenant Conclude and Agree to Enter into Co-partnership together and to become Co-partners and Joint Dealers in Making Burning and Selling the said porcelain Ware and All Other Sorts of wares which the said partners should Agree to make or Deal in and in the painting Japanning Gilding and Enamelling thereof

52

And in Gain and Loss According to the COVENANTS therein Mentioned during the said Term of Fourteen Years And the said William Jenkinson doth Thereby Grant Bargain Sell Assign and Set over unto the said William Nicklin five parts (the Whole into Twelve Equal parts to be Divided) and to the said William Littler two parts (to be Divided as aforesaid) of and in the said Leasehold premises Called Longton Hall with the Buildings Lands and premises therewith Demised of and in the said Household Goods purchased from the said Obadiah Lane Together with the Mills Clay Materials Moulds Modells and other Utensils of the said William Jenkinson and Mentioned in a Certain Schedule to the said Indenture Annexed AND WHEREAS there is a Covenant Contained in the said Recited Articles of Co-partnership that none of the said parties thereto shall Sell Assign or Dispose of his or their said Shares in the said Work or any part thereof without the Licence and Consent of the others of the said parties in Writing had and obtained for that purpose'.

The Second Agreement, dated the 25th of August 1753

'Between William Jenkinson of Longton Hall in the Parish of Stoke-on-Trent in the County of Stafford Gentleman of the First part William Nicklin of Newcastle under Lyme in the County aforesaid Gent of the second part William Littler late of Hanley Green in the Parish of Stoke upon Trent aforesaid but now of Longton Hall aforesaid Earth potter of the Third part and Nathaniel Firmin of the Parish of Saint Clement Danes in the County of Middlesex Water Gilder of the Fourth Part and Samuel Firmin Eldest Son and Heir Apparent of the said Nathaniel Firmin of the Fifth part.'

The agreement concerns the redistribution of shares. William Jenkinson sells his five shares and withdraws from the partnership. Nathaniel Firmin is mentioned as a new partner and buys three of these five shares. Samuel Firmin, his eldest son, is the fifth partner, but, being under age, he does not sign the agreement.

For the three shares which Nathaniel Firmin purchases he pays William Jenkinson nine hundred and forty-five pounds. William Nicklin and William Littler have one each of the remaining two shares which Jenkinson sells 'for divers other good causes and valuable considerations'.

The shares represent the interest in the work, the factory's furniture and stock of porcelain ware together with the household goods purchased from Obadiah Lane, all of which are to be the partners' property for ever; but a share of the leasehold premises would be theirs only during the remainder of the term of fourteen years.

If Littler were to die before the end of the said term of fourteen years his shares were to be transferred to 'Jane the now wife of the said William Littler'.

On Nathaniel Firmin's decease, if this should occur within the said term of lease, his shares were to be transferred to Samuel Firmin, his son. 'And Whereas the said Nathaniel Firmin the Father doth intend to give all the said Three parts or Shares to the said Samuel Firmin his Son in part of the provision Intended for him And the said Samuel Firmin being a person Much Approved of and very Agreeable to the said William Nicklin and William Littler.' If Nathaniel Firmin wished he could at any time, assign over his parts or shares 'of and in the said Works Goods Utensils Wares and Leasehold premises to the said Samuel Firmin the Son'. This would automatically make Samuel Firmin a partner even if the other two partners had not been parties to, or acquainted with, the assignment. Nathaniel Firmin could not, however, 'Assign Grant Convey or in any wise part with All or any of the said three Shares of and in the said Work Goods and premises or any of them or Any part thereof to any Other person or persons whomsoever (Except to the said Samuel Firmin) without the Licence and Consent of the Said William Nicklin and William Littler their Executors or Administrators under their Hands in Writing first had and obtained for that purpose'.

The agreement continues with its rather quaint legal phraseology. It goes on to state that William Jenkinson had paid to William Nicklin a proportionate share of the factory's outstanding debts; consequently, for this, and for other considerations already mentioned, William Nicklin and William Littler, their executors and administrators, covenant that they will 'from time to time and at all time hereafter save harmless and keep indempnified' both William Jenkinson and Nathaniel Firmin, their Executors and Administrators, and their property 'of and from all costs and charges in the Law or otherwise howsoever which they the said William Jenkinson and Nathaniel Firmin or either of them their or either of their Executors or Administrators shall or may be put unto of and Concerning the same (Except such debt or debts which may or have been Contracted by the said William Jenkinson alone on the said partnerships Account or wherewith the said partnership may be Charged by any Act or Contract of the said William Jenkinson heretofore made or done or hereafter to be made or done)'. The partners also indemnify William Jenkinson, his executors and administrators together with his and their possessions 'of and from all Costs and Charges in the Law or otherwise Howsoever that the said William Jenkinson shall or may happen to be put unto of and Concerning the Rent hereafter to become due for and in respect of the Lease aforesaid Granted by the said Obadiah Lane Of Longton

Hall and premises therein mentioned and from all Covenants Clauses and Agreements therein Contained which on the Lessees part and behalf are or ought to be paid done and performed'.

William Jenkinson then promises that he will not 'at any time or times during the remainder of the said Term of Fourteen Years in the said Recited Articles mentioned Either Alone or in partnership with any other person or persons directly or indirectly make or cause to be made of the said Porcelain or Ware in Imitation thereof which is now made at Longton Hall aforesaid and any Goods or Wares whatsoever and shall not or will not at any time or times hereafter during the remainder of the said Term of Fourteen Years directly or indirectly either by word or in writing or in any other manner whatsoever make known divulge or discover the Art or Secret of making the said Wares or of any of the Materials or Composition made use of therein in any manner howsoever'.

Finally the partners absolutely release, acquit, exonerate and discharge William Jenkinson from the co-partnership and William Jenkinson acknowledges receipt of two hundred pounds from William Nicklin under covenant from the first agreement. Then the document is signed by the four parties and endorsed with a receipt signed by William Jenkinson for the nine hundred and forty-five pounds paid him by Nathaniel Firmin. There is a further endorsement stating that: 'All accounts relating to the Co-partnership within mentioned shall be netted and stated twice in every year and not four times as mentioned in ye Articles of Partnership.'

Signed by William Jenkinson, William Nicklin, William Littler and Nathaniel Firmin.

Witnesses—William Hunt and B. Vaner.

The Third Agreement, dated the 1st of September 1755

The third agreement together with its two supplemental agreements tell the sad story of the financial failure of the Longton factory. This agreement is very lengthy and in a few places it is illegible even under ultra-violet light. Nevertheless it is an extremely interesting document and contains one or two important pieces of information (such as the mention by name of a Longton porcelain painter) and, in the supplemental agreements, a reference to a plan for moving the factory elsewhere.

The agreement is 'BETWEEN William Nicklin of Newcastle under Lyme in the County of Stafford Gentleman of the first part Samuel Firmin of the parish of St. Clements Danes in the County of Middlesex Buttonmaker of the second part William Littler of Longton Hall in the parish of Stoke upon Trent in the said County of Stafford Earth potter of the third part Robert Charlesworth of Bakewell in the County of Derby Clerk of the fourth part'.

The agreement begins: 'Whereas the said William Nicklin and Samuel Firmin are now and have been for several Years last and past at a very considerable expense in carrying on a Manufactory at Longton Hall aforesaid for making burning and enamelling a certain Porcelain Ware or Wares in imitation of Porcelain or China Ware and the said William Littler as manager thereof hath taken great pains therein and brought the same to a considerable degree of perfection And in Consideration of The Sum of Twelve Hundred Pounds of lawful British Money to be paid and advanced by the said Robert Charlesworth in manner herein after mentioned and of the trust and confidence the said Parties have in each other THEY the said William Nicklin Samuel Firmin William Littler and Robert Charlesworth have mutually covenanted and agreed and do by these presents covenant and agree each with the other of them his Executors and Administrators to enter into Co-partnership together and to become Co-partners in joint dealing as to profit and loss in the providing and procuring all proper materials for and also in the making burning and selling the said Ware And all other sorts of Wares which the said Partners shall agree to make and deal in And in the Painting Japanning Gilding and enamelling or ornamenting and making more perfect and saleable thereof and in Gain and loss according to the Covenants herein after mentioned during the Term of Ten Years.'

The parties agree that they will 'immediately on the execution of these presents and with as much expedition as the nature of the thing will admit of make known discover and lay open or cause to be made known discovered and laid open to the said Robert Charlesworth the whole art secret Mystery or invention of the said work in making burning bisketing glazing painting finishing and perfecting the said Porcelain Ware or Wares in imitation of Porcelain or China Ware and every Composition Matter and thing by them therein used and thereunto relating and all and every other Secret Mystery or Invention that they or any of them shall or may hereafter during the said Term obtain find out or invent in or about the making or perfecting any sort of Ware whatsoever with all convenient speed after the same shall be found out or invented by the said William Nicklin Samuel Firmin and William Littler or any of them'.

The arrangement of the twelve shares covered by the second agreement had been that William Nicklin had six parts, and Samuel Firmin and William Littler each had three parts. The third agreement states that the three shares owned by William Littler were held as one part in his own right and the other two parts were his only during his conduct and management of the factory. These partners agreed 'to convey to the said Robert Charlesworth one third part of the said Joint work And the said two shares of the said William Littler as conductor or manager of the said Work shall remain entire to him during such his management and to Jane his Wife in Case of his Death and of her surviving him and managing or causing to be managed the said Work as hereinafter mentioned and that the two shares last mentioned shall not be lessened by such Conveyance to the said Robert Charlesworth as aforesaid but that the said third part of the said work shall be made up and conveyed out of the said Six shares of the said William Nicklin of the said three shares of the said Samuel Firmin and the said one share of the said William Littler'.

To facilitate the new distribution of shares it was decided that the total shares should 'no more be called known or distinguished by the name of Twelve shares or parts But that the same shall be and are hereby divided multiplied and distinguished by the name of sixty shares'. Thirty of these shares were to be the property of William Nicklin, fifteen shares the property of Samuel Firmin and five shares the property of William Littler in his own right, and ten other shares the property of Littler and his wife or the survivor of them during his or her conduct and management of the factory.

William Nicklin then sells to Robert Charlesworth twelve of his thirty shares; Samuel Firmin sells him six of his fifteen shares, and William Littler parts with two of his five shares. For these twenty shares Robert Charlesworth promises that he will pay the sum of two hundred and fifty pounds to William Littler on or before the last day of October next ensuing as part of the said sum of twelve hundred pounds and that this was to be immediately used by Littler to discharge 'the several Debts mentioned and contained in a certain Schedule'[1] endorsing the agreement. Robert Charlesworth was also to advance to William Littler from time to time such sums as would be necessary or convenient for carrying on the manufactory, but not exceeding the sum of one hundred pounds in any one month, till the remaining nine hundred and fifty pounds would be fully paid. 'On or before the last day of October next' Robert Charlesworth agreed to advance one hundred and fifty pounds for defraying the expenses of the following month, and at the end of that month Littler had to furnish an account of the goods sold, wares made, and debts contracted in the same month; Robert Charlesworth would then pay the balance of such accounts so that the sum of one hundred pounds would be in the hands of William Littler at the end of each month for defraying the expenses of the following month.

[1] See p. 61.

In the event of a profit being made in any month the balance would be paid to Robert Charlesworth to be distributed among the partners according to their respective shares. However, all dividends were to be made with the consent of the major part of the partners at the time of settling accounts but no dividend was to be paid unless there would remain a balance of fifteen hundred pounds in cash and goods of which three hundred pounds was to be in ready cash to carry on the work. The major part of the parties would have the power before each dividend was appointed to put aside such further sums as they thought necessary for increasing the capital stock and for advancing the trade of the manufactory, provided that such sums did not exceed five hundred pounds in any one year.

In case William Littler and his wife were to die during the partnership the ten shares to which they were entitled for their conduct of the work were to go to the other partners. The executors and administrators of Littler and his wife or the survivor of them would only be entitled to ten parts of the stock in hand and wares then made and of all profits arising from the joint work on the day of the death of the survivor, and this was to include a proportionate share of all outstanding debts due to the factory at that time. For this purpose 'two indifferent persons' were to be chosen by the respective parties to appraise the value of the stock in hand.

The partners were to enter in their books 'true plain and perfect entries and accounts of their respective Bargains Sales receipts Payments and disbursements of and concerning the said Joint work And of all goods wares and merchandizes sold and delivered by any of them respectively and the several and respective days and times when such Goods were respectively sold and delivered and to whom the same and every or any part thereof have been or shall be sold and delivered and that the said William Littler shall make and keep a true plain and perfect account of all Goods wares and merchandize made at and bought for the Use of the said Work And the respective Name and Names of each and every person from whom the same and every part and parcel thereof have been or shall be bought And the respective time and times of making buying the same And that all Books of Accounts concerning the said partnership shall always during the Continuance thereof at Longton Hall aforesaid remain and be kept for their Joint Use in some convenient room or place in Longton Hall aforesaid And in Case the said Work shall be removed to any other place or places before the end of the said partnership then the said Books of Accounts shall be removed to and kept in such place or places where the said Work or works shall be carried on during the said partnership'.

The partners agreed that once in every quarter of a year, or more often if requested, they would send 'close copies' of their accounts to each other and 'settle the same in the best manner' possible. They or their proper agents were also to meet at Longton Hall once every year within one month of mid-summer, when they would draw up a balance sheet. Any profit resulting would be divided amongst them according to their respective shares provided sufficient capital was left for carrying on the work.

William Littler was to deduct one guinea a week out of the capital stock for the service and conduct of his wife in and about the said work, and he was also to deduct a further sum of one guinea a week for the service of John Hayfield, a painter employed in the said work. He was to make a reasonable and proportionable deduction out of this sum if John Hayfield neglected his work. If William Littler wanted to discharge John Hayfield and employ another person who had previously been approved of by the other partners then he could pay this other person the same weekly sum of one guinea. 'And the said William Littler may discharge not only the said John Hayfield but any other painter as often as he shall think fit (having from time to time the approbation of the parties to these presents or the major part of them of the person he shall employ as painter as aforesaid) and employing one painter and no more at the same time'. Littler promises that he and his wife will employ the utmost application and diligence in the conduct, business and management of the factory, and that they will not remove their habitation from Longton Hall without the consent of the other parties.

The other partners 'shall not be obliged to give any attendance or to act or work in their own persons in any Business relating to the said Co-partnership but at their Wills and pleasures nor charge the said partnership with any Sum or Sums of Money for or on account of such Business or work to be done as aforesaid by them or any of them unless such Business be undertaken by order of the majority of the said parties and then shall be allowed a reasonable satisfaction'.

Nobody was to be employed at the factory without the consent of the partners and the partners could desist from making or selling porcelain if this was agreed to by the major part of them. In the event of any disputes arising, they were to be settled by a panel of 'four indifferent persons'. None of the partners were to divulge the factory secrets to any other persons during the partnership, nor were they to trade in any other form of china ware or in the decorating of it without the consent of the other parties.

In case two of the partners were to disagree with the other two then the decision of the two who had the greatest shares of property or interest in the factory was to prevail and be binding in the matter in dispute.

On completion of the agreement William Littler was to make known all the factory processes to William Nicklin and Samuel Firmin, 'and every other secret mystery and invention which he shall or may hereafter obtain find out or invent in or about the making or perfecting any sort of Ware whatsoever'. If it were to happen that on or before the first day of September 1757, the produce or profits of the factory should amount to four thousand pounds in cash or good marketable wares which had already been sold to produce cash within six months of that time, then the said sum of twelve hundred pounds would be deemed a capital stock to be the property of the partners according to their respective shares. If, however, the sum of four thousand pounds could not be produced within that time then Robert Charlesworth was to be reimbursed with all the money which he had advanced and the remaining part of the produce was to become a capital stock for carrying on the work. For making certain of this repayment to Robert Charlesworth, in case this sum could not be realized, the other partners had agreed to sell him 'all and singular the Goods Chatels Leases Mills Moulds Utensils porcelain other Wares and Merchandizes Debts Credits Sum and Sums of Money due and owing' to them to be sold by him in order to raise sufficient money to reimburse him. Any surplus would belong to the rest of the partners.

If, upon trial or experience, it was found that the manufactory was not a gaining work after Robert Charlesworth had advanced six hundred pounds or more, and if the manufactured goods and good debts were not equal to the value of six hundred pounds or whatever sum Charlesworth had advanced, then it would be lawful for him to desist from advancing any further money and to draw out what he had already invested and be discharged from the partnership, assigning over his shares to the other partners. If this should happen William Littler would be discharged from the partnership within six months unless the other two partners or some other partner could produce six hundred pounds capital.

This present agreement was to cancel all other previous agreements concerning the joint work, but it was to be of no effect if a certain Francis Allen of Grays Inn did not 'on or before the twentieth of October next' effect a sufficient general release of all William Nicklin's 'property Interest claims divers debts and demands' which Francis Allen was claiming against William Nicklin or against the joint work.

The agreement is signed by the four partners (William Nicklin, William Littler, Robert Charlesworth and Samuel Firmin); Samuel Firmin's signature is witnessed by Francis Allen and J. Todd, and the other partners' signatures are witnessed by John Charlton and J. Sparrow

*   *   *   *   *

The schedule referred to in the third agreement is set out in full below.

Schedule referred to by the within written Deed

	£	s.	d.
Bruts for hay grass	3	3	0
Boulton for coals	44	6	0
Bagnall for materials		18	2
Hulm for brick work		17	2
Genders for smith work	1	5	0
Ward for broken glass	5	9	0
Smallwood for shop goods	5	3	7
Shaw for shop goods	4	3	3
Baddeley for boards	1	16	0
Russell for broken glass	12	7	4
Ridgway for shop goods	6	7	0
Mountford for work	12	15	0
Hollins for work	1	16	0
Bucknall for broken glass	1	2	6
Hays for broken glass	1	8	$9\frac{1}{2}$
Shipton for carriage	3	8	3
Smith of the furnace	3	10	0
Wages due for work	34	8	$4\frac{1}{2}$
Miss Shaw	15	0	0
Mr. Duesbury for work	—	—	—
Mr. Charlton for wages	19	4	8
Wages	4	10	6
For coals	1	5	6
Mr. Dickenson for treys etc.	2	5	0
Mr. Lane one year rent	25	0	0
Rent due to Miller at Longton	5	0	0
Collins stationery in London	2	13	5
Ralph Hammersley for brick	2	8	0
Mr. Littler	14	17	11
Mr. Derby for work	5	7	6
More to Mr. Smallwood	7	10	0
	249	6	11

The First Supplemental Agreement, dated the 20th of October 1756

This agreement acknowledges that Robert Charlesworth had advanced the sum of twelve hundred pounds in accordance with the third agreement and that a further sum of thirty-five pounds was due to him besides several other outstanding debts. All the money advanced had been expended and nothing remained to discharge the debts or continue the work, 'and the goods Manufactured are of very uncertain Value and by reason of many unforseen difficulties in making and ornamenting the same are not finished fit for market but almost All of them will yet require more expense and further hazard to make them marketable and the said Robert Charlesworth not thinking it proper or convenient to incur any further risque or expense in so precarious a Manufacture that after so long tryal has not yet Appeared to be a gaining work in which the rest of the parties by reason of their other engagements and respective business are either unwilling or unable to Assist did give Notice that he would draw out the Money Advanced by him according to the power reserved and granted to him for so doing'; but the other partners 'being of Opinion that in the present situation of their affairs the ruin of the whole work must be inevitable unless prevented by the further friendly assistance and support of the said Robert Charlesworth and that if he would advance the further sum of Three hundred pounds on credit of the said capital stock part of the goods might be finished and sold so as to raise money to go on with finishing the remainder and making fresh ware and a circulation of trade be established that might turn out to the Advantage of All parties and the said Robert Charlesworth being desirous to manifest his benevolence and the Uprightness of his intentions and to Act for the good of All parties and give the utmost satisfaction as far or even beyond what may Appear strictly prudent in compliance with their request Agrees to continue to employ the twelve hundred pounds already Advanced till the first day of September next ensuing'.

The next thirteen lines are practically illegible, but it appears that Charlesworth consented to advance a further sum of three hundred pounds for which he would charge an interest of thirty per cent. It was agreed that he should not advance more than a total of fifteen hundred pounds, and that if before the first day of September next the stock and capital were not of at least six hundred pounds value after Robert Charlesworth had been fully reimbursed with all the money which he had advanced together with the additional profit of thirty per cent and all other debts had been discharged, the partnership would be dissolved within one month unless a further sum of six hundred were advanced by some or all of the partners.

The agreement is signed by Robert Charlesworth, William Nicklin and William Littler in the presence of John Charlton, and also by Samuel Firmin in the presence of the same witness.

The Second Supplemental Agreement, dated the 1st of October 1757

This agreement states that the dissolution of the partnership had been prevented by Robert Charlesworth having on the 1st of October 1757 paid to William Littler six hundred pounds, of which four hundred pounds were paid back to him to cover future advances at the rate of one hundred pounds per month. The partners agreed that the work should be carried on during the remainder of the term of ten years but objection was raised to the hardship of paying Charlesworth thirty per cent for his money, and Charlesworth agreed to accept five per cent only, to be paid half-yearly out of the said stock for all money advanced or to be advanced by him. The interest on the twelve hundred pounds and three hundred pounds already advanced was to commence and be computed from the first day of October 1756, and the interest on the six hundred pounds was to be computed from the first of October 1757. It was agreed that if the present capital stock was not of the value of fifteen hundred pounds then the same should in the first place be made of that value and that no dividend would be made until such capital stock should be raised. Afterwards if the neat produce of the work should yearly amount to the sum of five hundred pounds then this would be paid to Robert Charlesworth as part of the money due to him unless he and the majority of the other partners should prefer to use this sum in advancing the work. If the produce were to amount to more than five hundred pounds yearly then this additional profit was to be divided amongst all the partners according to their shares. It would not be in the power of Robert Charlesworth to dispose of the capital stock or to put a stop to the work at any time unless it was plain that on the first day of October 1758, the whole capital stock was not worth more than one thousand pounds. If this should happen and the other partners refused to give a bond or obligation of the penalty of two thousand pounds to Robert Charlesworth within fourteen days that the capital stock should be of that value on or before the 1st of October 1759, then Robert Charlesworth could sell the capital stock and the partnership should be dissolved, unless Robert Charlesworth should think fit to continue the whole capital stock in the partnership during the remainder of the term. In the event of the other partners executing such a bond or obligation then the capital stock and the partnership were to be continued till the 1st of October 1759. If, however, any of the other partners should refuse or delay to execute this bond or obligation then those who refused would be totally excluded and debarred from all right property or interest of or in the present agreement.

If on the 1st of October 1759, the capital stock was less than one thousand pounds then the partnership would be dissolved, but if it was of that value the partnership was to be continued during the remainder of the term of ten years or so long as the capital stock remained at one thousand pounds.

In case Samuel Firmin should refuse to sign the agreement it was to be valid between the other partners, 'AND WHEREAS its agreed that the said Manufactory Shall be removed to Nottingham or Some other place NOW IT IS AGREED that the Expenses of making and Erecting kilns and Mills on Such removal and the Materials thereof and all other Expenses paid out thereunto Shall be Deemed as part of the said Capital Stock of One Thousand pounds and that Nothing herein or in the said Articles Contained in Regard to the Twelve Hundred pounds Three Hundred pounds and Six Hundred pounds or any part thereof Shall Affect the persons or Estates of the said William Nicklin Samuel Firmin and William Littler or any of them'.

This copy of the final supplemental agreement was signed only by Samuel Firmin in the presence of Thomas Appleyard.

Appendix B
NEWSPAPER REFERENCES

27th July 1752

Aris's Birmingham Gazette

Repeated a number of times. 'This is to acquaint the public that there is now made by William Littler and Co. at Longton Hall near Newcastle, Staffordshire, A Large Quantity, and great Variety, of very good and fine ornamental PORCELAIN or CHINA WARE, in the most fashionable and genteel Taste. Where all Persons may be fitted with the same at reasonable Rates, either Wholesale or Retale.'[1]

10th to 17th December 1754

Manchester Mercury

A dealer's advertisement announcing

'The first produce of the Factory at Longton near Newcastle in Staffordshire of Porcelain or China ware.'[2]

4th to 10th April 1757

London Public Advertiser

'To be Sold by Auction By MR. FORD, At his Great Room at the Upper End of St. James' Haymarket, on Tuesday 19th Instant, and the following Days. A Quantity of new and curious Porcelain or China, both useful and ornamental, of the LONGTON-HALL Manufactory, which has never been exposed to public View. As the Strength and Delicacy of the Composition, the Novelty of the Patterns, and the Beauty of the Execution have had the Approbation of the best Judges who have seen it, and the Proprietors having been at very great Pains and Expense in endeavouring after Perfection in this new Manufacture, they hope it will be thought worthy of Notice, and meet with the Encouragement of the Public, and they promise the Nobility, etc. who have desired to see it make its Appearance in this Manner, that the Whole shall be conducted with that Fairness and Honesty which they hope will merit their future Favours.

'The said Porcelain may be viewed on Saturday and Monday the 16th and 18th till the Time of Sale, which will begin each Day exactly

---

[1] Discovered by J. E. Nightingale.
[2] Discovered by Francis Buckley.

at Twelve o'Clock. Catalogues will be ready to deliver at Mr. Ford's, on Friday, the 15th inst. at 6d. each; the Money to be returned to those that are Purchasers.'

12th to 25th April 1757

From the 12th April to the conclusion of the sale on the 25th April, the following was the advertisement:

'A New and curious Porcelain or China of the Longton-Hall Manufactory, which has had the Approbation of the best Judges, and recommended by several of the Nobility to this public Method of Sale. Consisting of Tureens, Covers and Dishes, large Cups and Covers, Jars and Beakers, with beautiful Sprigs of Flowers, open work'd Fruit Baskets and Plates, Variety of Services for Deserts, Tea and Coffee Equipages, Sauce Boats, leaf Basons and Plates, Melons, Colliflowers, elegant Epargnes, and other ornamental and useful Porcelain, both white and enamell'd.'[1]

20th June 1757

Aris's Birmingham Gazette

Repeated two or three times.

'At the CHINA MANUFACTORY, by William Littler, at Longton Hall, near Newcastle, Staffordshire. There is now upon Sale all Sorts of CHINA, both useful and ornamental, as well plain blue and white Tea-China of all Sorts, Coffee-cans, Chocolate Cups and Saucers, Punch-Bowls and Mugs, as finely enamell'd and curiously modell'd Fruit-Dishes, Leaf-Plates, Sauce-Boats, and Variety of curious useful Ornaments for Deserts, with Figures and Flowers of all Sorts, made exactly to Nature, allow'd by the best Judges to be the finest in England, where all Gentlemen and Ladies who please to honour him with their Commands, may depend upon having the Favour greatly acknowledg'd and all Tradesmen who favour him with Orders, may depend upon having them faithfully executed by their most obedient humble Servant William Littler.'[1]

12th June 1758

Aris's Birmingham Gazette

'This is to acquaint the public that there is now to be Sold by William Littler and Co., at Longton Hall, near Newcastle in Staffordshire Great Variety of all Sorts of Useful and Ornamental PORCELAIN or CHINA WARE both Blue and White, and also Enamelled in the best and most lively colours; to wit, Services of Dishes and Plates, Tea and Coffee Equipages, and great Variety of Services for Deserts, Beautiful Essence Pots, Images, Flowers, Vases, etc. with fine Blue and White

[1] Discovered by J. E. Nightingale.

Ribb'd, Fluted, and Octagon Chocolate Cups and Saucers, Tea Sets, Etc. N.B. The LONGTON Porcelain is vastly improved, and is now allow'd by all Judges, to be the best made in England; the Prices are lowered, and are now very reasonable.'[1]

30th September to 3rd October 1758
London General Evening Post

'Longton China-Warehouse At the Corner of St. Paul's Church-Yard next Watling Street, London, is now open. Where may be had great variety of fine china ware useful and ornamental, both blue and white, and finely enamelled, viz. Cups and Saucers, Coffee Cups, Cream Jugs, Tea Pots, Bowls, Basons, Mugs, Decanters, Sauce Boats, compleat Tea and Coffee Sets, Chocolate Cups and Saucers ribbed, fluted, panelled and plain, with fine enamelled China Dishes and Plates, oval and round Leaf and fancy Patterns, curious Perfume Pots, Vauses, Figures and Flowers, etc. As likewise at the China Manufactory, near Stone, in Staffordshire. Orders sent to either of these Places will be gratefully received, and punctually complied with. N.B. Whereas several Persons have been so far misinformed as to fancy some of the Staffordshire Earthen Wares were the production of this Manufactory, they have expressed the greatest surprise at finding this to be the most beautiful China they ever beheld.'[2]

14th July 1759
London General Evening Post

'WHEREAS the Co-partnership lately subsisting between Messrs. BANKS and ROBERTSON, at the Staffordshire Warehouse in St. Paul's Church-Yard, was, by mutual Consent, dissolved the 24th of last Month; Mr. Robertson has, on his own separate Account, opened a large Warehouse at the East Corner of St. Paul's Church-Yard, next Watling-Street, and laid in a great Variety of China, Glass, Worcester, Staffordshire Ware etc. Where all Persons in Town and Country, who will be so kind as to favour him with their Commands, shall have the best and neatest Goods at the lowest Prices, wholesale or retail, and their Orders punctually executed by Their most obedient humble servant, John Robertson. St. Paul's Church-Yard. July 2nd, 1759.'[3]

9th June 1760
Aris's Birmingham Gazette

'Longton-Hall China Manufactory, in the County of Stafford, May

---

[1] Discovered by J. E. Nightingale.
[2] Discovered by A. J. B. Kiddell.
[3] Discovered by G. Wills.

23rd 1760. All persons are hereby desired to take Notice, that the Partnership between Mr. William Littler and Company, of Longton-Hall aforesaid, and Mr. Robert Charlesworth, is dissolved, pursuant to their Articles and Agreements, and that they are to give no Credit to the said William Littler and Company, on Account of the said Robert Charlesworth. And all Persons who are any Ways indebted to the said William Littler and Company, or have any Goods or Effects belonging to the said Company, in their Hands, are hereby required to deliver the said Goods and Effects, or pay the said Debts, into the Hands of M. Samuel Boyer, Attorney at Law, in Newcastle under Lyme, for the Use of the said Robert Charlesworth, who only has proper Power and Authority to recover and give a Release for the same.'[1]

30th June 1760

Aris's Birmingham Gazette

'Longton China Manufactory, June 24, 1760.

In answer to an Advertisement inserted in the Birmingham Gazette the 9th Day of June Instant, William Littler and Comp. think proper to acquaint the Publick, that it's not in Robert Charlesworth's Power to dissolve the Partnership therein mentioned, without Consent of the rest of the Partners; that the said William Littler and Co. are far from the Expectation of any Credit on the said Charlesworth's Account and are all very desirous to execute any proper Instrument for the Dissolution of the said Partnership, on having fair Accounts settled, and Damages paid by the said Charlesworth for his many Breaches of Covenant, and his late unjustifiable and illegal, tho' impotent and ineffectual, Attempt to put a Stop to the said Manufactory: And as the said Littler and Co. are a Majority of the said Partners, and have, by Articles of Partnership, not only an undoubted Right of disposing of the Partnership Effects, but in all Matters of Moment their Decision is final; therefore they give Notice to all Persons not to deliver any of the Goods or Effects belonging to the said Partnership to the said Robert Charlesworth, or either of them: And that all Gentlemen, Ladies, and others, may be fitted at Longton aforesaid, with much better Wares than ever, at reasonable Rates, by WILLIAM LITTLER and Co.'[1]

8th September 1760

Aris's Birmingham Gazette

'London July 17, 1760. It having been advertised in the Birmingham Gazette the 30th of June last, that the Works At Longton Hall China Manufactory, in the County of Stafford were still carried on by

[1] Discovered by A. J. B. Kiddell.

Part of the Company, and that the Partnership was not dissolved, as had been represented in another Advertisement, published in the aforesaid Paper, on the 9th of the same Month; now in Order to reconcile the said opposite Notices, as far as regards myself, and lest it should be insinuated or apprehended, that I have at present any Concern in carrying on the said Works, I hereby declare, that I esteem the Partnership therein as dissolved the 23rd of May last, pursuant to a Notice sent me by Mr. Robert Charlesworth (one of the said Partners) for that Purpose. And I do therefore hereby give Notice to all Persons not to credit the said Company, or any of the Parties concern'd in the said Works, on my Account. Witness my Hand

SAMUEL FIRMIN'[1]

8th September 1760

Salisbury Journal

'To The Nobility, Gentry, Shopkeepers and others. Mr. Samuel Clarke sworn Exchange-broker of Cheapside London will sell by Publick auction, on Tuesday the 16th inst. and the four following Days at the Great Sale Room at the Sun at Fisherton adjoining the city. The Genuine large and valuable stock of the Longton Porcelaine China Factory, which, as the partnership is dissolved, will be sold without reserve or the least addition; containing upwards of ninety thousand Pieces of the greatest variety of Dresden Patterns in rich enamel'd, pencil'd, Blues and Gold; as Figures and Flowers, mounted in Chandeliers, Essence Jars, Beakers, Vases, and Perfume Pots, magnificent Dessert Services, sets of Bowls, Mugs, Dishes and Plates, ornamented with Columbines and Central Groups, Tea Coffee and Toilet Equipages, of elegant patterns superbly furnished, equal to a national Factory, so eminently distinguish'd, with a profusion of useful and ornamental articles. Particulars will be mentioned in the Catalogue which may be had at the place of Sale. The whole may be viewed the Friday, Saturday and Monday preceding the Sale, which begins each day at ten in the morning and at five in the Evening.'[2]

[1] Discovered by A. J. B. Kiddell.
[2] Discovered by Norah Richardson.

INDEX

1. *Jacobite Group. 'Snowman Family'.*
Mr. and Mrs. Sigmund Katz Collection. See page 27

2A. *Cupid at Vulcan's Forge. 'Snowman Family'. Height $7\frac{1}{4}$ in.*
Owner unknown. See page 27
2B. *Cupid at Vulcan's Forge. 'Snowman Family'. Height 5 in.*
Fitzwilliam Museum. See page 27

3A. *Turkeycock Candlestick. 'Snowman Family'. Height* $7\frac{3}{8}$ *in.*
Fitzwilliam Museum. See page 28
3B. *Heron. 'Snowman Family'. Height* $4\frac{1}{4}$ *in.*
Rous Lench Collection. See page 28
3C. *Seated Pug Dog. 'Snowman Family'.* 1750 *incised on base.*
Length 2 in. Rous Lench Collection. See page 27

4A. *Ceres. 'Snowman Family'. Height* $6\frac{5}{8}$ *in.*
Bernard M. Watney Collection. See page 31
4B. *'Winter', 'Snowman Family'. Height* $5\frac{1}{4}$ *in.*
Bernard M. Watney Collection. See page 27
4C. *'Summer'. 'Snowman Family'. Height 5 in.*
Fitzwilliam Museum. See page 27

5A. *Figure of Lawyer. 'Snowman Family'. Height* $6\frac{3}{4}$ *in.*
Bernard M. Watney Collection. See page 29
5B. *Littler's blue-and-white stand with leaf moulding and gilt decora-*
tion. Early period. Length $11\frac{1}{8}$ *in.*
Bernard M. Watney Collection. See page 30

6A. *Littler's blue-and-white two handled basket. Early period.*
Length 6¾ in.
Cecil Higgins Museum, Bedford. See page 30
6B. *Littler's blue-and-white taper stick. Early period. Height 4½ in.*
Rous Lench Collection.

7A. *Three piggins painted in colours and 'Littler's blue'.*
Early period. Length 3¼ in.
Mrs. J. Smith Collection.
7B. *Scallop shell tray painted in 'Littler's blue'. Early period.*
Width 4¾ in.
Bernard M. Watney Collection.

8. *Ewer and Basin painted in colours and 'Littler's blue.' Early period.*
Basin diameter 10½ in.
Rous Lench Collection. See page 30

9A. *Littler's blue-and-white tureen and stand.*
Crossed 'L' mark. Early period. Height 6 in.
Mr. and Mrs. Sigmund Katz Collection. See page 30
9B. *Bowl and cover painted with the early palette.*
Rous Lench Collection.

10A. *Ceres Salt. Painted in colour. Early period. Height* $7\frac{2}{5}$ *in.*
British Museum. See page 32
10B. *Early Salt in Colours.*
Courtesy of Messrs. Tilley and Co.

11A. *Chamber pot. Painted with orange banded pattern. Height 5 in.*
Rous Lench Collection. See page 31
11B. *Early straight sided mug with thick crazed glaze. Decorated in*
colours with orange-red predominating. Height 5 in.
Bernard M. Watney Collection. See page 30

12A. *Teapot, cover and fluted stand. Decorated with 'Quail Pattern'*
in colours. Early period.
Courtesy of Charles Woollett. See page 31
12B. *Undecorated fluted cup and saucer with early paste and glaze.*
Bernard M. Watney Collection.

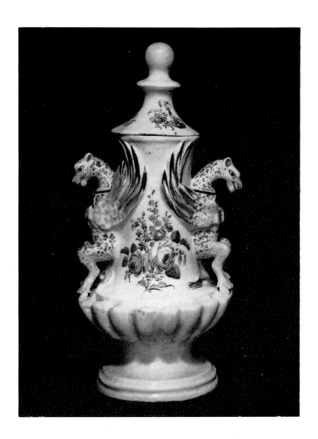

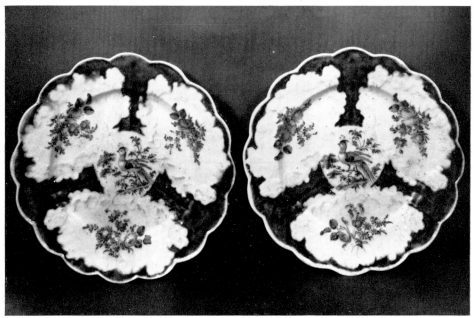

13A. *Pseudo-heraldic vase and cover showing early flower sprays in colour. Height $12\frac{1}{2}$ in.*
Rous Lench Collection.
13B. *Pair of moulded scallop edged plates painted with 'Littler's blue' and flower sprays in colour. Early period. Diameter 7 in.*
Rous Lench Collection. See page 24

14. *Small scallop edged plate with broad 'Littler's blue' border and early bird and butterfly group. Diameter 6 in. Bernard M. Watney Collection. See page* 31

15. *Coffee pot with child's head knop and typical early flower sprays.*
Height 10⅜ in.
Bernard M. Watney Collection. See pages 30 *and* 31

16. *Littler's blue-and-white coffee pot of six lobed silver shape. Traces of oil gilding. Crossed 'L' mark. Height $8\frac{1}{4}$ in. Bernard M. Watney Collection. See page 30*

17. *Fluted mug of heavy early paste. Decorated in colours with birds
and flowers. Height 6 in.
Bernard M. Watney Collection. See pages* 31 *and* 34

18A and B. *Gallant and Lady formed as candlesticks. Early period.*
Height 8 in.
Rous Lench Collection. See pages 32 and 34
18C. *Ceres candlestick. Decorated in colours. Applied flowers and*
looped twigs on base. Height 10 in.
E. A. Rees Collection. See page 32

19A. *Blue-and-white moulded cream jug with typical early Longton handle.*
Mr. and Mrs. Sigmund Katz Collection.
19B. *Blue-and-white leaf moulded cream boat. Early period.*
Holburne of Menstrie Museum, Bath. See page 30
19C. *Littler's blue-and-white chamber candlestick. Early period.*
Rous Lench Collection.

20. *Moulded jug with ground of 'Littler's blue' showing unusually elaborate factory decoration including white enamel scroll work. Transitional period. Height 7½ in. Victoria and Albert Museum. See page 30*

21. *One of a pair of ornate vases with strawberry knops on covers.*
Scenes taken from Pillement's engravings. Painted in colours.
Transitional period. Height 10¾ in.
Victoria and Albert Museum. See page 34

22A. *Six sided bottle in underglaze powder blue with traces of oil gilding and applied decoration. Transitional period. Height 5 in. E. A. Rees Collection. See page 33*

22B. *Powder blue bottle decorated with Chinese scenes. Transitional period. Height 5 in. E. A. Rees Collection. See page 33*

22C. *Melon shaped powder blue teapot. Transitional period. Dr. and Mrs. Statham Collection. See page 33*

23A. *Blue-and-white armorial plaque. Height 5⅜ in.*
Mr. and Mrs. Sigmund Katz Collection.
23B and C. *Blue-and-white sauce boat and a biscuit teapot waster from*
the Longton site, both moulded with the same floral pattern.
Hanley Museum. See page 24

24. *Silver shaped sauce boat with bird painting in colours and almost matt surface. Another example is in the Reading Museum. Transitional period.*
C. W. Dyson Perrins Collection. See page 33

25A. *Ornamental fruit shaped boxes showing an apple, plum and lemon*
on a leaf moulded stand. Transitional period. Diameter 7 in.
Mr. and Mrs. Sigmund Katz Collection. See page 33
25B. *Silver shaped sauce boat. Painted in colours.*
Another example in the Katz Collection.
Dr. and Mrs. Statham Collection.

26A, B and C. *Arbour Group with supporting candlesticks. Transitional
period. Height of candlesticks, boy $8\frac{3}{4}$ in., girl 10 in.
Mr. and Mrs. Sigmund Katz Collection. See page 34*

27A. *Teapot with flower painting in a free style. Unusually elaborate handle and apple shaped knop on cover. Another example differently decorated in the Fitzwilliam Museum.*
Transitional period. Height 3⅝ in.
Thomas Scholes Collection. See page 34
27B. *Pair of coffee cans with salt glaze type of coloured decoration. Twig and bud handles. Transitional period. Height 2⅜ in.*
Rous Lench Collection. See page 34

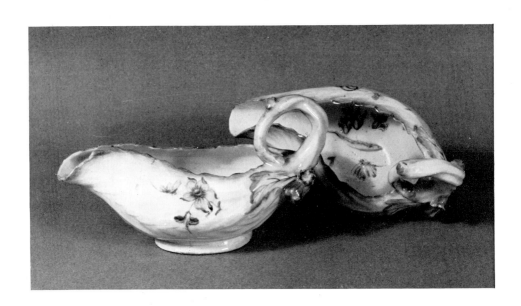

28A. *Pair of leaf shaped sauce boats decorated with green edges and*
soft enamel colours. Transitional period. Length 7½ in.
Bernard M. Watney Collection. See page 34
28B. *Early strawberry plate with insect and bird decoration in colours.*
Transitional period.
Dr. and Mrs. Statham Collection. See page 34

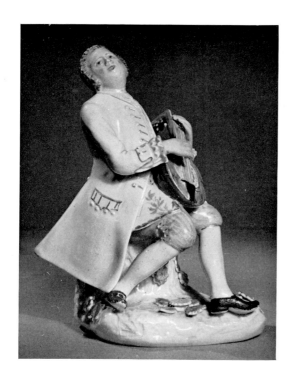

29A. *Lute Player with gilt buttons and shoe buckles, model after a Käendler original. Middle period. Height* $6\frac{3}{4}$ *in.*
David Goldblatt Collection. See page 37
29B. *Flute Player. Another example in the MacAlister Collection. Middle period.*
Mr. and Mrs. Sigmund Katz Collection. See page 38

30A, B, C and D. *'The Four Seasons'. With typical early flat faces. Middle period. Height about 4½ in. Fitzwilliam Museum. See page 38*

31A. *Fruit seller decorated on the base with large open roses and leaves.*
Middle period.
Mr. and Mrs. Sigmund Katz Collection. See page 38
31B. *Naked boy on horseback. Simple flat base. Middle period.*
Height 6⅖ in.
British Museum. See page 38

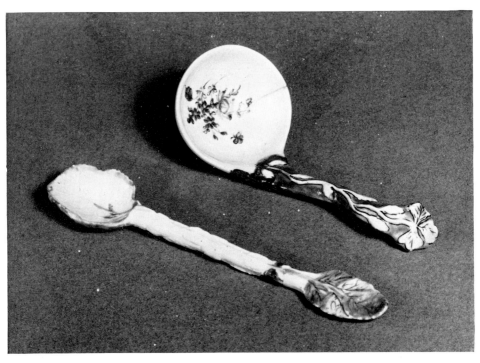

32A. *Ornamental box in the shape of a lemon with applied flowers on the cover. Middle period. Length $2\frac{3}{4}$ in.*
Dr. and Mrs. Statham Collection. See page 39
32B. *Small ladle and spoon with leaf moulded handles. Early and middle periods. Length of spoon $6\frac{1}{2}$ in.*
Dr. and Mrs. Statham Collection.

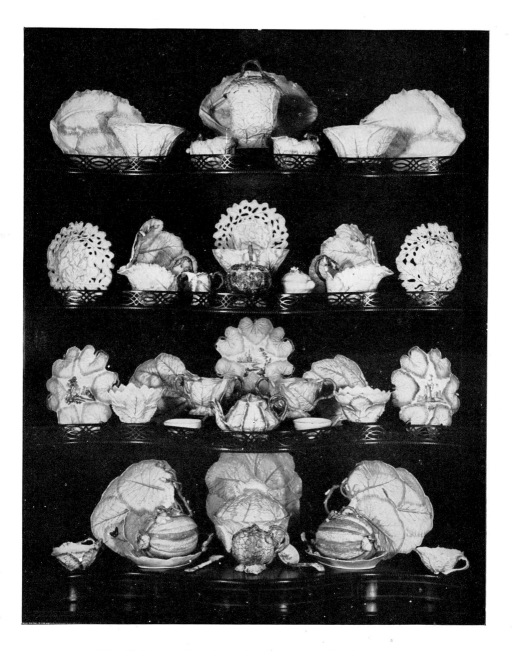

33. *Cabinet of leaf moulded wares. Middle period.*
Dr. and Mrs. Statham Collection. See page 35

34A. *Figure of girl gathering spring flowers. Yellow hat and skirt, and white apron; collar and cuffs painted to represent ermine. Middle period.*
Height 5 in.
Mr. and Mrs. Sigmund Katz Collection.
34B *and* C. *Pair of seated figures holding flower sprays. Emblematic of Spring and Summer. Copied later at Derby. Middle period.*
Height 4¾ in.
Mr. and Mrs. Sigmund Katz Collection, See page 38

35A. *Pair of pugs seated on their haunches with curled tails. Underglaze manganese decoration. Eyes and collars in underglaze blue. Unmarked. Middle period. Height 3½ in. and 3⅝ in.*
Mr. and Mrs. Sigmund Katz Collection. See page 37
35B. *Cow cream jug with underglaze manganese decoration and blue painted eyes. Cover moulded with honey bee. Middle period.*
Height 4⅞ in.
Ernest Allman Collection. See page 37

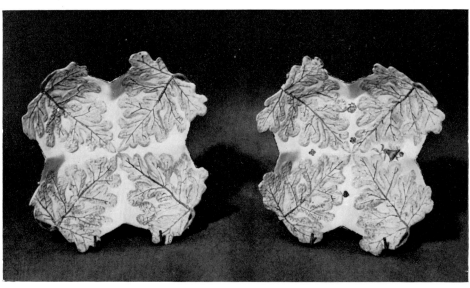

36A. *Leaf dish. Decorated by the 'Castle Painter'. A similar example in the Rees Collection bears an impressed crossed 'L' mark. Middle period.*
Mr. and Mrs. Sigmund Katz Collection. See page 37
36B. *A pair of fine leaf dishes. Middle period. Width 8 in. Courtesy of Albert Amor Ltd. See page 35*

37A. *A flower seller decorated in coloured enamels. Middle period.*
Mr. and Mrs. Sigmund Katz Collection.
37B. *Companion to flower seller. Middle period.*
Courtesy of Albert Amor Ltd.

38A. *Openwork leaf stand decorated with yellowish green.*
Middle period.
Mr. and Mrs. Sigmund Katz Collection. See page 35
38B. *Leaf tray in colour. Middle period. Length* $6\frac{1}{8}$ *in.*
Mrs. J. Smith Collection. See page 35

39. *Openwork leaf moulded stand. Factory decorated with birds and flower sprays. Middle period.*
Seattle Art Museum. See pages 35 *and* 37

40A. *Seated figure of Harlequin as a bagpiper. Middle period.*
Height 5¼ in.
Mr. and Mrs. Sigmund Katz Collection. See page 38
40B. *Columbine playing a hurdy-gurdy. Skirt decorated with playing*
cards and flowers. Middle period. Height 5 in.
Rous Lench Collection. See page 38
40C. *Masked figure of Harlequin. Coat decorated with playing cards*
and breeches chequered in the Meissen Manner. Middle period.
Height 5 in. Rous Lench Collection. See page 38

41A. *Two handled leaf moulded sauce boat decorated in colours.*
Middle period.
Dr. and Mrs. Statham Collection. See page 35
41B. *Tulip teapot. Coloured enamel decoration.*
Green rustic handle and spout. Middle period.
Rev. C. J. Sharp Collection. See page 40

42. *Figure of Turk. Buttons and sword hilt picked out in gilt.*
Middle period. Height 7¼ *in.*
Victoria and Albert Museum. See pages 34 *and* 44

43. *Turk's companion. Head dress and sleeves decorated with dark underglaze blue. Another coloured version is in the Katz Collection. Middle period. Height 7¼ in.*
Mrs. J. Smith Collection. See pages 34 and 44

44A. *Bird candlestick. Raised crest and black face.*
Middle period. Height 5½ in.
Courtesy of Sotheby and Co. See page 39
44B. *Pair of melon tureens with bird knops. Middle period.*
Height 6 in.
Mrs. Isaacson, U.S.A. See page 39

45A. *Theatrical reading figure. Middle Period.*
Mr. and Mrs. Sigmund Katz Collection. See page 38
45B *and* C. *Pair of reading figures. Decorated in pale colours with pink*
predominating. Middle period. Heights $3\frac{3}{4}$ *in. and 3 in.*
E. A. Rees Collection. See page 38

46A. *Strawberry Plate decorated in colour. Middle period.*
Holburne of Menstrie Museum, Bath. See page 35
46B. *Leaf moulded teapot with green rustic handle. Middle period.*
Height 4¼ in.
Dr. and Mrs. Statham Collection. See page 40

47A. *Vase with perforated top. Spiral moulding.*
Painted in colours. Middle period. Height 7½ in.
E. A. Rees Collection.
47B. *Moulded sauce boat. Salt glaze pattern. Pencilled decoration.*
Middle period. Length 8 in.
Bernard M. Watney Collection. See page 37

48A. *Two octagonal cups and saucers. Blue-and-white decoration.*
Middle period.
Bernard M. Watney Collection. See page 40
48B. *Sauce boat. Coloured decoration with flower sprays and insects.*
Middle period. Length 8 in.
Dr. and Mrs. Statham Collection.

49A. *Rustic teapot decorated by the 'Castle Painter'. Middle period.*
Courtesy of Charles Woollett. See page 40
49B. *Moulded jug with green rustic handle. Strawberry leaf and*
auricula plant moulding and flower sprays. Middle period.
Mr. and Mrs. Sigmund Katz Collection. See page 35

50. *Figure of piper and dog. Middle period. Height 5¾ in.*
Dr. and Mrs. Statham Collection.

51. *Figure of infant artist with palette representing 'Painting' from the*
'Arts'. Yellow drapery. Middle period. Height 5½ in.
Dr. and Mrs. Statham Collection. See page 38

52. *Figure of an infant Bacchus. Drapery painted in madder red.*
Middle period. Height 5 in.
Dr. and Mrs. Statham Collection.

53. *Figure of a farmer with bird's nest. Unusual floral decoration.*
Middle period. Height 5¾ in.
Victoria and Albert Museum.

54A. *Pineapple teapot. Scales painted red-brown with green edges.*
Rustic handle and spout painted yellow and green. Middle period.
Rev. C. J. Sharp Collection. See page 40
54B. *Cream jug moulded with strawberry leaves. Middle period.*
Height 3 in.
Dr. and Mrs. Statham Collection. See page 35
54C. *Cream jug. Wide lip and simple handle. Painted in colours by the*
'Trembly Rose Painter'. Middle period. Height 3 in.
Bernard M. Watney Collection.

55A. *Figure of butter seller from the Longton series of market folk.*
Middle period.
Mr. and Mrs. Sigmund Katz Collection.
55B *and* C. *Figures of gardener and his companion. Scrolls on bases*
picked out in puce. Middle period. Heights $4\frac{3}{4}$ *in. and* $4\frac{1}{4}$ *in.*
Mr. and Mrs. Sigmund Katz Collection.

56A. *Dancing figure similar to figure on pot-pourri vase covers.*
Middle period. Courtesy of Albert Amor Ltd. See page 39
56B. *Figure of a Putto representing 'Music' from the 'Arts'.*
Lyre painted brown and gilded. Middle period.
Mr. and Mrs. Sigmund Katz Collection.
56C. *Figure of Putto representing 'Summer'. Drapery decorated with*
dark underglaze blue. After a Meissen original. Middle period.
Height 4½ in. Geoffrey Cavendish Collection.

57A. *Figure of abbess. Cloak and hood painted black with pink lining.*
Habit white with gilded edging. Middle period. Height 5 in.
David Goldblatt Collection.
57B *and* C. *Pair of cooks. Typical large open roses and flat leaves*
decorating high rocky bases. Middle period. Height 6 in.
Mr. and Mrs. Sigmund Katz Collection. See page 38

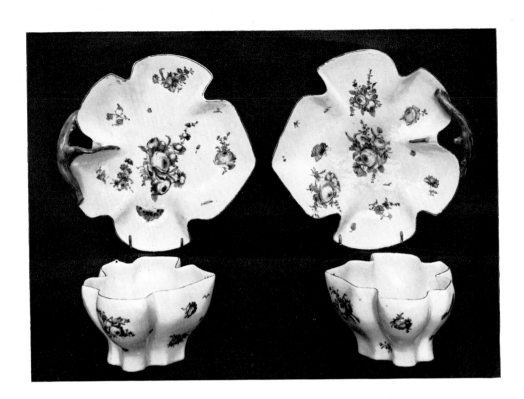

58A. *Pair of leaf shaped basins and stands. Coloured flower sprays by the 'Trembly Rose Painter'. Middle period.*
Rous Lench Collection. See page 35
58B. *Cup and saucer. Flower sprays by the 'Trembly Rose Painter'.*
Purplish pink predominating. Middle period.
Bernard M. Watney Collection. See page 40

59A. *Figure of Hercules and the lion on separate stand. Another example with a stand in the Rous Lench Collection. Middle period. Height 7½ in.*
E. A. Rees Collection. See page 38
59. *Pair of pigeon tureens finely decorated in colours. Middle period. Mr. and Mrs. D. MacAlister Collection. See page 39*

60A. *Cylindrical mug of slightly tapering form. Goose pattern derived*
from Chinese original. Middle period.
Courtesy of Albert Amor Ltd.
60B. *Bowl. Shape inspired by Chinese original. Root and flower pattern.*
Middle period. Height 2⅝ in.
Mrs. Harnan Collection, U.S.A. See page 41

61A *and* B. *Two enamelled candlestick groups, emblematic of Spring*
and Autumn. Several undecorated examples exist. Middle period.
Ex Eckstein Collection. Courtesy of Sotheby and Co.
61C. *Figure of flower seller. Male companion to cabbage seller.*
Plymouth adopted this model later. Middle period. Height 7¾ in.
Cecil Higgins Museum. See page 38

62A. *Three blue-and-white mugs showing varieties of handles.*
Middle period.
Bernard M. Watney Collection. See page 40
62B. *Two cream boats in blue-and-white. Unusually moulded bases.*
Middle period.
Bernard M. Watney Collection. See page 40

63A. *Pair of rococo vases decorated mainly in purple. Middle period.*
Victoria and Albert Museum.
63B *and* C. *Pair of equestrian figures after Meissen models by Kaendler.*
Middle period. Heights 8 in. and 8½ in.
Victoria and Albert Museum. See page 44

64A. *Figure of two Putti feeding goat with grapes representing Autumn.*
Middle period. Height 5¼ in.
Mr. and Mrs. Sigmund Katz Collection. See page 38
64B. *Blue-and-white spoon tray showing 'folly' pattern.*
Middle period. Length 6⅜ in.
Bernard M. Watney Collection. See page 40

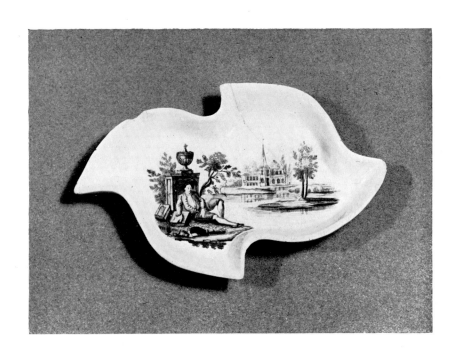

65A. *Spoon tray decorated in colours by the 'Castle Painter'.*
Length 6⅝ in. Middle period.
Bernard M. Watney Collection. See page 37
65B *and* C. *Pair of candlesticks. Sheep and goat models.*
Middle period. Height 5⅕ in.
British Museum.

66A. *Bell shaped mug. Fine chinoiserie decoration in colour.*
Middle period. Height 6½ in. Mrs. J. Smith collection. See page 41
66B *and* C. *Pair of figures in fancy dress representing Lovers with a*
birdcage. Middle period. Heights 9½ in. and 10 in.
Mr. and Mrs. Sigmund Katz Collection and Cecil Higgins Museum, Bedford.
See pages 39 and 43

67A. *Peach shaped cup with rustic handle.*
Shape derived from K'ang Hsi Bridal Cups. Middle period.
Rous Lench Collection. See page 35
67B. *Figure of a Gallant playing with a dog.*
Middle period. Height 9 in.
E. A. Rees Collection. See page 38

68A. *Blue-and-white peach shaped cup. Middle period.*
Victoria and Albert Museum. See page 35
68B. *Figure of lady in fancy dress as a shepherdess playing with a dog.*
Middle period. Height 8¾ in.
Late Lord Fisher Collection. Fitzwilliam Museum. See page 38

69A. *Blue-and-white cup and saucer both marked with the letter 'k' in underglaze blue. Middle to late period.*
Bernard M. Watney Collection. See page 40
69B. *One coloured and two blue-and-white bottles.*
Late period. Heights 2¾ in. and 5¼ in.
Bernard M. Watney Collection and Mrs. J. Smith Collection.

70A. *Two blue-and-white cream jugs, one showing twin basket moulding.*
Middle to late period.
Bernard M. Watney Collection. See page 25
70B. *Large blue-and-white sauce boat with twin basket moulding and*
drip catcher below the spout. Middle to late period. Length $7\frac{1}{2}$ *in.*
Victoria and Albert Museum. See page 39

71A. *Barrel shaped teapot decorated with continental scenes by the 'Castle Painter'. Middle to late period.*
Mr. and Mrs. Sigmund Katz Collection. See page 36
71B. *Butter dish and stand painted with flower sprays. Middle period.*
Rous Lench Collection.
71C. *Blue-and-white moulded dish. Middle to late period.*
Hanley Museum. See page 37

72A. *Barrel shaped teapot. Enamelled with brightly coloured birds.*
Middle period. Height $4\frac{1}{2}$ in.
Bernard M. Watney Collection. See page 41

72B. *Straight sided mug with root pattern and paeony decoration.*
Late period. Height $4\frac{3}{4}$ in.
Bernard M. Watney Collection. See page 41

75. 'The Dancers', sometimes described as 'The Lovers'. Rococo base
picked out in purple. Late period. Height 10¾ in.
Late Lord Fisher Collection. Fitzwilliam Museum. See page 43

74A *and* B. '*The Musicians*'. *Late period. Heights* 11$\frac{3}{4}$ *in. and* 11$\frac{3}{8}$ *in.*
Late Lord Fisher Collection. Fitzwilliam Museum. See page 43

75. *'Winter' from a set of infant seasons. Later copied by Plymouth.
Impressed 'K' mark. Late period. Height $5\frac{3}{8}$ in.
Victoria and Albert Museum. See page 44*

76A. *Blue-and-white barrel shaped teapot. Acorn knop.*
Middle to late period.
Mr. and Mrs. Burrell Collection. See page 41
76B. *Transfer printed cream jug. Pastoral scene.*
Signed 'Sadler Liverp.' Late period.
Cecil Higgins Museum, Bedford. See page 25

77. *Figure of Britannia holding portrait medallion of George II.
French trophies at the side. Decorated at Liverpool with two coloured
transfers over-painted with enamels. Late period. Height $11\frac{1}{4}$ in.
David Goldblatt Collection. See page 44*

78. *Figure of Minerva. Simple square base. Grey and gilt cuirass and
yellow skirt. Late period. Height 7½ in.
David Goldblatt Collection. See page 44*

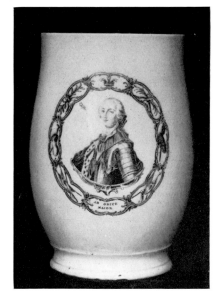

79A. *Transfer printed mug bearing the coat of arms of the FitzSteven family. Late period.*
Dr. Knowles Boney Collection. See page 43

79B. *Transfer printed bell shaped mug showing portrait of Prince Charles Edward. Motto 'Ab obice major'. Late period.*
Dr. Knowles Boney Collection. See page 43

79C. *Pair of straight sided mugs, transfer printed with the coat of arms of Mark Hildersley, Bishop of Sodor and Man. Late period.*
Manx Museum. See page 43

80A. '*Europe*'. *One of the four continents. Elaborately decorated in colours. Late period. Height* 12⅝ *in.*
Temple Newsam, Leeds. See page 45
80B. '*Asia*'. *Late period. Height* 12¼ *in.*
Temple Newsam, Leeds. See page 45
80C. '*Africa*'. *Late period. Height* 12⅞ *in.*
Temple Newsam, Leeds. See page 45
80D. '*America*'. *Late period. Height* 13¼ *in.*
Temple Newsam, Leeds. See page 45